FIN KENNEDY

Fin is a graduate of the MA Writing for Performance programme at Goldsmiths College, London. His first play, *Protection*, was produced at Soho Theatre in 2003, where he was also Pearson writer-in-residence. His second play, *How to Disappear Completely and Never Be Found*, won the 38th Arts Council John Whiting Award, the first time in forty years that an unproduced play had won. It was subsequently commissioned by Samuel West for Sheffield Crucible and enjoyed a sell-out run, transferring to London in 2008. It has also been produced in Australia, New Zealand and the United States, and is becoming a firm favourite with amateur and student groups around the UK.

Fin's first play for teenagers, *Locked In*, a hip-hop musical about pirate radio, was produced by Half Moon Young People's Theatre in 2006 and 2008, and toured nationally. His second play for Half Moon, *We Are Shadows*, toured during autumn 2007. 2008 also saw Fin's first radio commission, *Caesar Price Our Lord*, for BBC Radio 4, which was transmitted in September of that year.

For the past four years he has been writer-in-residence at Mulberry School for Girls in Tower Hamlets, London, where he is co-founder of Mulberry Theatre Company, for whom the plays in this volume were written. *Mehndi Night* (2007), *Stolen Secrets* (2008) and *The Unravelling* (2009) all premiered at the Edinburgh Fringe Festival, while *The Urban Girl's Guide to Camping* premiered at Southwark Playhouse in 2010.

As well as writing plays, Fin also has many years of experience teaching playwrighting at secondary, sixth-form, undergraduate and postgraduate levels. He has worked for schools, youth clubs, local authorities and theatre education teams in inner London and beyond, and is also a visiting lecturer at Goldsmiths College and Boston University.

Other Titles in the Series

Fin Kennedy

THE URBAN GIRL'S GUIDE TO CAMPING

and other plays

Mehndi Night

Stolen Secrets

The Unravelling

The Urban Girl's Guide to Camping

NICK HERN BOOKS

London

www.nickhernbooks.co.uk

A Nick Hern Book

The Urban Girl's Guide to Camping first published in Great Britain in 2010 as a paperback original by Nick Hern Books Limited, 14 Larden Road, London W3 7ST

All photographs (including front cover) by Giles Moss giles@digitalchild.co.uk
Production posters and logo designed by Brett Noble noblehobbit@yahoo.co.uk
Cover design by Ned Hoste, 2H

Typeset by Nick Hern Books, London
Printed and bound in Great Britain by CLE Print Ltd, St Ives, Cambs PE27 3LE

A CIP catalogue record for this book is available from the British Library

ISBN 978 1 84842 120 2

Contents

Foreword

When first looking for a writer-in-residence for Mulberry
Theatre Company, I knew we would need a playwright who not
only had the talent to bring their own voice and creativity to the
work, but also was able to listen with care and sensitivity to
new young voices. In Fin Kennedy, we found such a talent. He
has written in his Introduction of his pleasure at being
introduced to a new environment; in return, he has empowered
our students, by bringing craft, skill and inspiration to
dramatising their authentic voices. This has created a string of
successful productions and facilitated a series of extraordinary
performances, and in doing so, created a platform for a group
otherwise little represented in British theatre.

This publication is a tribute to the collective creativity and
artistic endeavour of many people at the school; students, staff
and artists-in-residence. There is a belief at Mulberry School in
the power of the arts to enrich education and enhance our lives.
I am deeply grateful to Vanessa Ogden, Head Teacher, for
inspiring and encouraging our work, and to Sarah Dickson,
Director of Arts Specialism, for her unwavering support.

I am delighted that this volume of plays will ensure that
something very important to our school will now be more
widely shared. It is a testament to the courageous and
triumphant spirit of all the young women of Mulberry, both past
and present, whose determination is heard so clearly in these
pages.

Jill Tuffee
Deputy Head, Mulberry School

Introduction

When Jill Tuffee, then Head of Expressive Arts at Mulberry
School for Girls, first approached me in the foyer of Half Moon
Young People's Theatre in 2004, little did I realise that our
conversation would lead onto a creative collaboration that would
last for the rest of that decade, and produce six new plays in as
many years. I was writer-on-attachment at Half Moon, and Jill's
group had just finished a day working with a short play of mine,
B Minor[1]. Jill's offer to come into school to collaborate on
something further was both an opportunity and a challenge. I had
never written anything specifically for teenagers before (though
Half Moon's use of *B Minor* was the first step in developing one
of my first plays for them, later christened *Locked In*[2]).

Mulberry is a comprehensive on the Commercial Road in Tower
Hamlets. Due to its catchment area, its student population is
made up of ninety-eight per cent Muslim students of
Bangladeshi heritage, mostly second or third generation. They
are a disarming mix of East and West, traditional and modern –
and absolutely the rightful heirs to the rebellious spirit of East
London, that has run through each community that has settled
there over the centuries. They couldn't have been more different
from me, a white middle-class playwright from Brighton and
Winchester. But we got on surprisingly well, they took me into
their trust, and were soon overflowing with anecdotes, local
news, gossip and revelation – all material that went into our first
play together, *East End Tales*[3] (to which *Stolen Secrets* in this
volume owes a debt).

The direct-address storytelling style that I developed for this
first group, and which recurs in varying forms in every play in
this volume, had several motivations behind it. The first was
purely practical; teenagers have busy lives and many demands
on their time. If you write individual parts for each of them,
when availability issues arise it's difficult to rehearse. But an
indeterminate chorus without specific characters can be

delivered as a shared narrative with as many or as few actors as you get that week, the lines simply redistributed among them.

The second reason was so that the plays could be performed almost anywhere, with minimal set or props, and free from naturalistic constraints in depicting 'reality'. Direct address allows the action to move fluidly through space and time – just a few words and the illusion is created, the scene set. Moreover, such a style solves one of drama's perennial difficulties – how to externalise the internal. A chorus of narrators can be endowed with a certain omniscience about the thoughts and feelings of the subjects of their stories.

But finally, and perhaps most importantly, it is about capturing something of the essence of teenagers – the effervescent tall tales, the excitable outrage, the delight in gossip. Teenage actors *want* to acknowledge their audience. Indeed, unlike naturalistic writing for this age group, which often produces an awkward, faux-soap-opera style of acting, direct-address storytelling actively plays to young actors' strengths. And, as we discovered when we began to take shows to the Edinburgh Festival, audiences love it too. One critic described their 'untutored naturalism, refreshingly honest and unrestrained', while another the 'glee and openness that you cannot help falling for'. My writing takes its cue from the corridors of Mulberry School itself.

My relationship with Mulberry became a formal arrangement in 2007, when the school achieved specialist status in Arts[4] and, along with several other artists-in-residence, I became a permanent, part-time member of staff. Jill Tuffee, supported by the school arts team, set out an extraordinarily ambitious vision: putting creativity in all its forms at the heart of the school – of which my work, and this volume, is merely one part. There is also Mulberry Films, Mulberry Radio and a wealth of other projects and residencies taking place across departments. The common philosophy is that everyone learns – students, staff and artists. So one day I might be learning from the teaching skills of experienced Drama or English teachers, the next they might be learning from me by attending my Staff Playwriting Course. Or I might teach the students about dramatic structure while they teach me about Bengali culture, the latest slang, or sayings from the Qur'an.

It's an approach that underpins every play in this volume. A separate introduction to each play will explain more about our evolving process, but the overarching lesson I have learned is that it is the artist-in-residence's responsibility, over time, to encourage students beyond making obvious choices, and into areas of genuinely original creative thought. As Sabina says in *The Urban Girl's Guide to Camping,* 'What you discover will be amazing. What you discover will be yourself.'

Mulberry Theatre Company has now produced more of my work than any other theatre company. Far from monopolising my attention – I still regularly write plays for adults – these two sides of my work have become two sides of the same coin. But the school also affords me a blank canvas of its own, a nursery in which to try out new dramatic forms, and to get to know and develop characters who are totally unlike me. My plays – not to mention my life – are undeniably the richer for it.

I'd like to take this opportunity to offer my thanks to everyone at Mulberry School who has welcomed me with such enthusiasm over the past four years. I'm so proud of what we have achieved together, and thrilled that this volume is being published. It is a fitting tribute to just what can be achieved with creative thinking, institutional support, and a spirit of bold collaboration.

Fin Kennedy
May 2010

---

1. This play was published in *Brand Literary Magazine* in 2006 and is available for free download at tinyurl.com/35upo4l (performance rights reserved)

2. This play toured nationally in 2006 and 2008. More here: tinyurl.com/38vfzra

3. Previously published by Methuen as part of *Six Ensemble Plays for Young Actors*

4. More information on this scheme can be found here: tinyurl.com/34almpr

MEHNDI NIGHT

Author's Note

The first of our Edinburgh Festival plays, *Mehndi Night* marked
the first time in British theatre history that a play had been
written entirely for and about British Bangladeshi women. This
was very much a result of the way in which the play was
developed, with ten committed fifteen-year-olds over several
months; their desire to create a play for a mainstream adult
audience about the women of their community, and the effect of
the modern world on their relationships with one another. I owe
a debt of gratitude to my co-tutor on this project and director of
the play, Julia Voce, whose nurturing of the groups'
performance skills allowed us to put the young actors into
character for up to forty-five minutes at a time. The
psychological depth to the characters in such a large-cast play,
not to mention the raw material for dramatic scenarios, could
not have been developed in any other way. But perhaps most of
all, I am indebted to the ten young women who shared their
culture with us with such openness, when the whole idea of
artists and students collaborating in this way was still such an
experiment. They led us through their world and we helped
them give it a dramatic form. It was a privilege to be allowed
into their lives.

Mehndi Night was first performed on 2 August 2007 at Venue 45, Edinburgh, with the following cast:

NILUFA	Marjana Rahman
LUBLY	Khadija Sharaz Khanom
HASINA	Nabarupa Deb
SALMA	Sabina Aktar
MARIAH	Thania Sultana
RIPA	Rubena Begum
KOLPHANA	Farhana Hussain
ALEYA	Aklima Begum
LEYLA	Fahmina Begum
SHULÉ	Rebeka Yasmin
Director	Julia Voce
Designer	Kollodi Norton

4

Characters

NARRATORS

BRIDE'S FAMILY
NILUFA, *twenty-four, secretary in a law firm, bride*
LUBLY, *forty-four, housewife, bride's mother*
HASINA, *sixty-four, Tesco worker, bride's grandmother*
SALMA, *twenty-six, housewife and part-time primary school-teacher, bride's big sister*
MARIAH, *sixteen, college student, bride's little sister*
RIPA, *twenty-two, estranged middle sister, a rapper and DJ*
KOLPHANA, *forty, dinner lady, bride's auntie*

BRIDEGROOM'S FAMILY
YAHYA, *twenty-six, art teacher, bridegroom (offstage)*
ALEYA, *fifty, housewife and nursery volunteer, bridegroom's mother*
LAYLA, *eighteen, university student, bridegroom's sister*

OTHERS
SHULÉ, *fifty-three, housewife, neighbour of family*

Note

Translations throughout the text are marked 'Sylheti', the dialect of Bengali from the Sylhet region of Bangladesh – which is the most widely spoken in East London

NARRATORS. This is a story about us
    Our sisters
    Mums
    Aunties
    Cousins
    We're East London
    Third generation
    Bengali girls
    You don't hear from us all that much
    But believe me
    We can be
    LOUD.

    Born here
    From there
    Not quite fitting anywhere
    We're the square pegs of the world
    Eastern look
    With an East End attitude
    And a faith that's in the news
    Man, that's a lotta things to juggle
    And you thought being Scottish[1] was hard.

    But raise your eyes
    Check the sky
    See them constellations?
    That's us
    We're your stars
    Your fortune
    Your future
    Because the next step
    In twenty-first century
    Multicultural UK
    Is not just to coexist
    In isolated toleration
    Chattin crap bout immigration

It's to take an interest
Recognise that we are blessed
To know each other
So listen up, yeah.

Today will be a celebration
Of marriage
Love
And good relations
Consider it your education
Cos we're like your in-laws
Tied together
For ever
A bit of a pain in the arse at times
But you love us really
And we're glad you're here
Yeah
At our mehndi
Even if you don't know what that is
You're gonna find out.

Mehndi, yeah
Is what you call henna
But it's more than what Madonna does to herself, innit
Mehndi is essential for any wedding
A good design means good luck
The more intricate and beautiful
The more your groom loves you
Aaaah
So us girls all get together
The night before the wedding
For a mehndi party
I spose it's what you'd call a hen night
Except without the drinking
Yeah, no one pukes
Or gets arrested
But stuff happens
Oh, yeah
Stuff happens alright...

Okay, enough
Yeah, you'll give the play away

Alright, let's meet the family
Yeah!

The actor playing NILUFA *steps up.*

The others sculpt her as they speak, perhaps putting some finishing touches to her costume or make-up.

First up
We got the bride
Nilufa Begum
Blushing
Shy
Sweet like mishti[2]
Loves her sisters
Loves her mum
Quiet
But strong
And clever
This girl always gets what she wants
To us she's managed the impossible
A husband she loves
Who everyone approves of
A career of her own
And she keeps Dad happy
Jealous?
We are
Hey, didn't she kiss some boys she shouldn't have?

NILUFA. Shut up!

NARRATORS. Yeah, Mum'll hear!
  Anyway that was ages ago.

NILUFA. Yeah.

NARRATORS. All in the past
  Or is it?
  Don't stir!

They clap their hands and NILUFA *comes to life.*

Salaam aleikum[3], Nilufa.

NILUFA. Oh my God I'm so nervous.

NARRATORS. Happy mehndi, sweetheart
It'll be fine
Have some chai
Go and relax.

NILUFA *goes and sits down*.

The actor playing LUBLY *steps up*.

The cast go through the same process of shaping her.

Okay, next
We got Lubly
That's Nilufa's mum
She's a nice lady
So long as you stay on her good side
This handbag has been known to swing
A mother and housewife
All her life
Mother to three girls
Four –

LUBLY. Three!

NARRATORS. Ssh, we don't mention her, innit
Sorry
Spends her days
Making tandoori
Singing ghojols[4]
Watching Bangla TV
And smoking shisha
When her husband's out
Blessed with daughters
Or burdened, some would say
Her life is their life
And so she dreams
Dreams of the fields of Bangladesh
Dreams of the day they are all married off
And she can finally relax
Retire
Grow rice
And grow old.

They clap their hands and LUBLY *comes to life.*

LUBLY. Subhan-Allah![5] Zanoor shanti nai![6]

NARRATORS. Welcome, moizi[7]
    Take a seat
    Everything is just how you wanted it
    And the guests are starting to arrive.

LUBLY. Hai hai.

    LUBLY *goes and sits down.*

    The actor playing HASINA *steps up.*

    The cast go through the same process of shaping her.

NARRATORS. Now we're going back in time
    Swirling through the mist
    To a time when every single one of us
    Was just a twinkle in this lady's eye
    It's Hasina
    Grandma
    Dad's mum
    Where this aaaall started
    She's everyone's favourite
    Hunched over now with arthritis
    But don't be fooled
    Cos inside
    She's the youngest
    Naughtiest
    Cheekiest one of us all
    Hasina loves
    Loves
    Loves
    Shopping!
    Parties!
    Dancing!
    Music!
    Driving way too fast!
    Living in the present
    And not caring bout the past
    Make-up!

High heels!
R'n'B!
Jogging round the flat!
Talking loud
And shoplifting.
Hasina's where it's at.

They clap their hands and HASINA *comes to life.*

HASINA. Where are all the pretty boys?

NARRATORS. It's a mehndi, Grandma
     Girls only.

HASINA. We need music! And dancing!

NARRATORS. All in good time
     Hardly anyone's here yet.

HASINA. I will be here dancing when you are all in bed!

NARRATORS. It's true
     She's a goer.

HASINA *goes to sit down.*

The actor playing SALMA *steps up.*

SALMA. Make me into Salma.

NARRATORS. Alright.

The actor playing MARIAH *steps up.*

MARIAH. And I want to be Mariah.

NARRATORS. Okay
     Hold still.

*The cast go through the same process of shaping them, both
at once this time.*

In the background, HASINA *prepares* LUBLY *and* NILUFA
for their grand entrance.

Salma
And Mariah
Are Nilufa's sisters.

Not only is there ten years between these two
There's a whole world
Salma's serious
Serious Salma
Works in a primary school
Scaring all the kids
This girl is a mum-in-waiting
The strict kind
Happily married
So far as we know
For a year or two now
Cooking
Cleaning
Bossing us around
Helping Mum suggest husbands
I mean, as if she has any taste in men!
Not meaning no disrespect to her husband or nuffing.

Mariah on the other hand
Yeah, Mariah
Right little tearaway, innit
Staying out late
Cotching[8] with mates
Only goes to college to pick up a date
Swears like a trooper
And smokes the odd fag.

MARIAH. Ah shut up, man, I sound like a slag.

NARRATORS. Yeah, alright
She ain't a slag
But she wouldn't mind being a Wag.

MARIAH. Yeah!

NARRATORS. What's a Wag?
Footballer's wife, innit.

MARIAH. Now that's what I call a career.

NARRATORS. Right then, we're done
Get over there.

They clap.

SALMA *and* MARIAH *go upstage and join the mehndi.*

The actor playing KOLPHANA *steps up.*

KOLPHANA. Can I be Kolphana?

NARRATORS. Man, are you mad?
    That's Dad's sister
    Bride's auntie
    A right old bag.

The actor playing SHULÉ *steps up.*

SHULÉ. If you're gonna do her, I'd better be Shulé.

NARRATORS. Yeah, I spose
    That's the neighbour from hell
    These two are best mates
    Though you never would tell
    They'll gossip and bitch and turn on each other
    Fighting like dogs
    Or sister and brother
    Then turn round and smile
    And plait each other's hair
    Grown-ups are weird, innit
    Only thing they got in common
    Is a love of GOLD.

They drape SHULÉ *and* KOLPHANA *in gold.*

KOLPHANA. A bride who gets no gold, gets no love.

NARRATORS. Then, the whispering starts.

SHULÉ. I don't like to gossip.

KOLPHANA. Nor me, go on.

SHULÉ. Lubly's husband's lost his job.

KOLPHANA. No!

SHULÉ. I'm serious.

KOLPHANA. Did you hear about Ripa?

SHULÉ. No!

KOLPHANA. Apparently she's back.

Everyone claps and SHULÉ *and* KOLPHANA *freeze.*

NARRATORS. Right, that's enough out of you two
Save it, please
No one really wants em here
But not inviting em ain't an option
They'd drag us through the mud.

Everyone claps again and SHULÉ *and* KOLPHANA *come to life.*

Everyone greets them warmly.

Shulé!
Kolphana!
Lovely to see you!
Thanks so much for coming!

KOLPHANA / SHULÉ. We wouldn't miss it for the world.

KOLPHANA *and* SHULÉ *join the others at the mehndi.*

The cast make rude gestures once their backs are turned.

The actors playing ALEYA *and* LEYLA *step up.*

There is just one actor left to shape them now – the actor playing RIPA.

Last but not least
We got the scariest guests of the lot
It's the groom's family, innit
Aleya's his mum
And Layla's his sister
Now this is one clever family, swear down
Intellectuals, y'get me
Cos Layla's at university
Doing 'Sociology'.

LAYLA. It's the study of human society and the fundamental laws of social relations, actually.

ALEYA. Buchossni?[9]

RIPA. Yeah, alright, I knew that.

ALEYA. Education is the key, every child must study.

RIPA. Seen seen, just chill out, yeah.

ALEYA. Do not tell me to chill, it is quite cold enough in this country.

RIPA. For real, man.

LAYLA. Only by exposing the channels of power that keep us oppressed will we ever challenge the hegemony.

RIPA. Not in Tower Hamlets, mate
Here
Eat that.

She gives LEYLA *a samosa.*

ALEYA. Wait a minute.

RIPA. What?

ALEYA. Who are you?

LAYLA. Yeah, which one are you?

RIPA. That's a good point
I guess you're just going to have to wait and see.

RIPA *winks, claps her hands, and music starts.*

RIPA *fades into the background.*

From now on, she becomes invisible to everyone present.

All the other women begin a traditional song-and-dance routine.

During the routine, NILUFA *enters ceremoniously, with* LUBLY *and* HASINA *at her side.*

LUBLY *takes* NILUFA *to her throne, sits her down and feeds her fruit.*

HASINA *goes to join in the dancing.*

HASINA (*to* MARIAH). How you do those sexy move? Teach me the sexy move!

MARIAH. Like this, Grandma!

HASINA *busts a few slinky moves.*

KOLPHANA (*to* HASINA). Subhanallah! Mother, you have no dignity! She is so embarrassing, I can't watch.

A circle forms with MARIAH *and* HASINA *in the middle.*

MARIAH *teaches* HASINA *her dance moves.*

The song and dance ends and everyone claps.

Some music remains playing quietly.

Now that it is quieter, we can also hear the rain outside.

Everyone helps themselves to food and drink and talks among themselves.

RIPA *steps forward again.*

RIPA. After the dancing, the gossip starts. Shulé and Kolphana like to judge the mehndi itself, innit.

SHULÉ. *Vegetable* samosas?

KOLPHANA. Yes, they have scrimped on the food.

SHULÉ. Times are tough for them, I heard.

KOLPHANA. My mehndi was ten times bigger.

SHULÉ. Mine too.

KOLPHANA. A hundred times.

SHULÉ. Her husband doesn't earn what he used to. Look at the fruit. Pathetic.

KOLPHANA. And have you seen the bride's sari?

SHULÉ. I know. Cheap.

KOLPHANA. I remember being poor. Never again.

SHULÉ. And this weather!

KOLPHANA. It's a stupid time of year to hold a mehndi.

RIPA. While Leyla and Aleya try their best *not* to judge their in-laws-to-be.

LEYLA. I think Yahya chose the best sister, don't you, Mum?

ALEYA. Leyla, not now.

LEYLA. He did.

ALEYA. Leyla!

LEYLA. Salma never smiles and Mariah never stops.

ALEYA. I wish *you'd* stop.

LEYLA. They're like the two extremes – Bangladesh at one end, Tower Hamlets at the other. Nilufa's somewhere in the middle.

ALEYA. Must you always analyse?

LEYLA. It's what you taught me.

ALEYA. Try not to judge.

LEYLA. I'm not.

ALEYA. Leyla, please. Not today. We are all family now.

RIPA. While sisters Salma and Mariah can't agree on nothing. The decade between em like a thousand years.

SALMA. I can't believe Mum let you wear that.

MARIAH. What's wrong with it?

SALMA. Look at the back.

MARIAH. Yeah, I look well buff, innit.

SALMA. You look cheap.

MARIAH. Well, you look old.

SALMA. You should cover up more.

MARIAH. You should shut up more.

SALMA. You cheeky little sod!

MARIAH. Yeah, yeah.

SALMA. Don't speak to me like that!

MARIAH. Man, can we change this music?

SALMA. This is Bengali music.

MARIAH. I want R'n'B.

SALMA. That is slut music.

MARIAH. Little slow jam or suttin. Nice.

SALMA. You talk like a street urchin.

MARIAH. *Grandma* likes slow jam.

SALMA. Grandma's completely insane.

RIPA. And as for poor Mum, well, she never could relax, innit.

LUBLY. Hai hai. My last day with my daughter.

HASINA. It is a happy day.

NILUFA. It's okay, Mum, I'm not going far.

LUBLY. I am losing you.

HASINA. She is growing up.

NILUFA. I'll be two streets away.

HASINA. Becoming a woman.

NILUFA. Stop it, Grandma.

HASINA. You are.

LUBLY. That's alright for you to say. You *gained* a daughter
   when I married Hassan.

HASINA. And did I ever stop you seeing your mother?

NILUFA. Grandma's right, Mum.

HASINA. Yes, it is a happy time. One less to worry about.

LUBLY. I have to worry, it is my job.

HASINA. Two down, two to go.

LUBLY. One! One to go!

NILUFA. Mum –

LUBLY. Do not even mention her name. I have three daughters,
   understand? Only three.

HASINA. Lubly, we should celebrate what God has given us.

LUBLY. Excuse me. I must see to our guests.

   The guests are chatting among themselves.

LUBLY *takes a tea urn and goes to top up everyone's chai.*

As she does so, she sees RIPA *like a ghost.*

She stops and stares at her.

Everyone else freezes.

RIPA (*to audience*). On the night I left she looked at me just like that. Hard. Cold. Raised her head. Looked me straight in the eye and said:

LUBLY. You're dead. You are dead to me.

Everyone comes back to life.

LUBLY *moves on, topping everyone up.*

Everyone queues up round the bride to feed her fruit.

HASINA *applies mehndi to* NILUFA*'s hands.*

RIPA. Next, everyone has to feed the bride. It's sort of a blessing. But of course it's also a chance to dish out some free advice.

Everyone gives NILUFA *their advice as they take their turn feeding her.*

SALMA. A woman's priorities should be Allah, children and work. In that order. Husband comes last. In your house, you are Queen and he is your servant. Never let him forget that.

SHULÉ. You *must* learn to cook and clean, Nilufa. It is what men want. You can borrow my mop any time.

KOLPHANA. May he always buy you gold. You can never have enough. Gold is the measure of a man's love, and a woman's happiness.

HASINA. I pray for great-grandchildren. I will teach them sexy dancing. But do not wait too long! Although I intend to live for ever, one can never be sure what God is planning.

ALEYA. Welcome to our family, daughter. We are blessed to receive such an angel into our home.

SALMA. Always respect your mother-in-law. She is your new mother.

LUBLY. Hai hai.

   ALEYA *prods* LEYLA.

LEYLA. I welcome you as a new sister. We will always look after you. I can lend you lots of interesting sociology books if you ever get bored.

RIPA (*to audience*). You have no idea how much I want to be standing in that line. But it's like I'm pressed up against glass, looking in. The rain pouring into me like bullets. They don't even know I'm here.

MARIAH. I'll miss you, Nilufa.

NILUFA. Oh sis, come here.

MARIAH (*tearful*). Be free. Enjoy yourself. Never let him hold you back. Make sure he loves you as much as you love him.

LEYLA. Of course he does, that's why they're getting married.

SALMA. Pah, love! You two are teenagers, what do you know about love?

LEYLA. Quite a lot, actually.

   ALEYA *quietens* LEYLA.

MARIAH. I know it's the most important thing in the world!

SHULÉ. No, security is the most important thing in the world.

KOLPHANA. Security through gold.

HASINA. Nonsense!

ALEYA. Education is the key.

LEYLA. Yeah, understanding how the world works.

SALMA. And trust in Allah.

HASINA. Yes, but family! Family is the eggs.

LEYLA. What?

HASINA. Family binds everything together.

LEYLA. You mean like an agent of socialisation.

HASINA. No, like an egg.

MARIAH. And fun!

HASINA. Yes, having fun with your family.

MARIAH. And parties!

SALMA. The world is nothing without Allah. You half-naked party women are having fun but what about your souls?

KOLPHANA. Well said.

HASINA. Oh, leave the girl alone.

NILUFA. Mum?

> LUBLY *stops pouring*.

> Mum, who is right?

> LUBLY *thinks*.

LUBLY. They are all right. All these things make us who we are. Culture is not a pick-and-mix. Life is not a buffet. It is a samosa. Every ingredient in harmony with every other. Then carefully wrapped and sealed from prying eyes.

> *The older women applaud.*

RIPA (*to audience*). She's always said that. Ever since we were little.

> LUBLY *shoots* RIPA *a look*.

SHULÉ. Well said.

KOLPHANA. Your mother is a wise woman.

RIPA (*to audience*). Wasn't so wise with me. She hasn't changed. (*Shivers.*) I'm cold.

> LUBLY *shoots* RIPA *another look*.

RIPA (*to* LUBLY). Yeah. I'm your conscience, Mum.

MARIAH. I want a love marriage like Nilufa.

LUBLY. Hai hai. Love is more complicated than you could possibly understand, child.

MARIAH. I'm not a child!

ALEYA. A respect marriage is better.

SALMA. Men just want to be mothered, that's the secret. They're big babies.

KOLPHANA. People under the age of forty cannot love anyone but themselves.

LUBLY. You can say that again!

LEYLA. That's not fair, we love our mums.

ALEYA. Bless you.

MARIAH. Yeah, and our sisters. (*Looks at* SALMA.) Well, most of em.

SALMA. Moizi, that is so true, arranged *is* better. What does anyone know when they're silly and young? Best leave it to people who understand these things.

SHULÉ. There's more to talk about if a marriage is arranged.

KOLPHANA. Yes, you have to get to know each other.

SHULÉ. Love marriages run out of conversation after a few years. You spend the rest of your lives watching Bangla TV together in silence.

ALEYA. Family love is the best. It is like a tree. Natural, solid and strong. Always there.

KOLPHANA. It's true. Romantic love is different. It is not thunder and lightning, like in Bollywood. It comes in little bits, like a rope which you weave together over many many years. Having picnics together in summer, giving you lifts to the shops, rubbing your toes in the evening. That is love. It is not instant, like cheap coffee. Love is learnt. Love is earnt.

ALL. It's true. / Moizi's right. / You gotta earn it. / Good old Kolphana.

HASINA. Bullcrap!

KOLPHANA. Excuse me?

HASINA. Kolphana is bullcrap!

KOLPHANA. Mother!

LUBLY. I am so sorry, she's had too much chai.

HASINA. Nonsense! Chai is the reason you are all here! Your grandfather worked on the tea ships to England! We met in Chittagong and we fell for each other straight away! Our love was like chai, sweet and spicy and intense. It filled our souls from the moment we saw each other.

KOLPHANA. Mum, you are so embarrassing!

HASINA. None of you would be here except for romantic love! It exists, like the chai you are drinking. It is what we all live for.

ALL. I'm so sorry about her. / What an outburst. / I'm so embarrassed. / Ignore her, she's old. / I love you, Grandma. / If that's how it was for her, who are we to argue? / Do you think it really was like that? / Grandad never mentioned it.

RIPA (*to audience*). Man, I miss Grandma. She's like the family spirit, right there. I'm outside looking in, shivering with the cold. Everyone older, but sort of the same. The familiar smell of the house. It's been four years.

Thunder rolls gently.

The rain outside steps up a notch.

During the following exchanges, RIPA *slips offstage quietly.*

SALMA. We shouldn't be talking about these things. It's embarrassing.

LUBLY. Salma is right. Enough of this, Hasina.

HASINA. This is your family history, you should show more respect.

MARIAH. I'm with Grandma, man. Her and Granddad were like Romeo and Juliet!

LUBLY. Romeo and Julia did not exist!

KOLPHANA. Yes, that is silly drama, pay no attention.

SHULÉ. Written by a white man.

KOLPHANA. Yes, an ugly white man.

SHULÉ. With no hair.

KOLPHANA. Exactly. What would he know about love?

HASINA. More than you.

KOLPHANA. Shut up, Mother.

HASINA. Miserable child.

LUBLY. Ladies, please.

NILUFA. I like Shakespeare.

SALMA. Yes, but you're weird.

LUBLY. Salma! Don't talk to your sister like that at her mehndi!

SALMA. Sorry.

NILUFA (*to* SALMA). Just cos you weren't allowed to do drama.

LUBLY. Nilufa!

NILUFA. She wasn't!

SALMA. I was no good.

NILUFA. You used to get As.

LUBLY. Your father put a stop to all that.

SALMA. Quite right too. What use is drama?

LUBLY. We came to see you in that show. You were rubbish.

MARIAH. No she wasn't!

NILUFA. Yeah, you weren't *that* bad, were you?

　　SALMA *stuffs fruit into* NILUFA*'s mouth to stop her
　　speaking.*

KOLPHANA. At home we play drama with the children.

SALMA. Yes, and in my school.

KOLPHANA. See? It is for babies. Who else likes drama? No
　　one.

SHULÉ. I like drama.

KOLPHANA. You're a housewife.

HASINA. I like drama.

KOLPHANA. You're insane.

NILUFA. Everyone likes drama.

SALMA. Don't speak with your mouth full.

MARIAH. Yeah, what about Bollywood?

SHULÉ. Yes, and I love a good telenovela.

ALEYA. It's true, these things can cheer you up.

LUBLY. Not me.

MARIAH. Nothing cheers *you* up.

> LUBLY *clips* MARIAH *round the ear.*

> Ow!

LUBLY (*to* MARIAH). Any more of your cheek and you can stand outside in the rain.

LEYLA. You can gain confidence doing drama.

ALEYA. Leyla, shush.

LEYLA. What? I want to be a lawyer, so it's useful.

LUBLY. Hai, there are no doctors and lawyers in my family. That is what we need and I have failed. How can all these teachers look after me? Learning, learning – rubbish! I have learned all there is to know about the world. Now I need money. Money for my old age.

HASINA. Nonsense! You are as old as you feel!

LUBLY. I feel older than the Earth.

HASINA. Earth is old, but it is not mad.[10]

MARIAH. You can act, can't you, Grandma! Remember all those games when we were little?

> HASINA *does an impression of a monster and scares* MARIAH.

KOLPHANA. What is this arty-arty thing in your family, Lubly? Where does it come from? Not my brother, that's for sure.

LUBLY. I have no idea, I despair.

HASINA. It comes from me of course. You and your brother were so boring, Kolphana. I wanted fiery sparky children! (*Indicates* MARIAH.) But I suppose these things skip a generation.

KOLPHANA. Oh, shut up, Mother. It is haram[11] for women to behave like this.

HASINA. Oh, have some betel nut[12] and let your hair down.

ALEYA. Yes, times are changing. If acting and music bring food to the table and don't put off a husband, then it's okay.

SHULÉ. As a last resort, if you are starving.

KOLPHANA. Finances should be the priority.

MARIAH. Actors get rich.

SALMA. It's not our culture, this music and drama.

MARIAH. It's *my* culture.

KOLPHANA. No it isn't.

SALMA. Law is better, everyone needs law.

MARIAH. Then why aren't you a lawyer?

LUBLY. She wasn't clever enough.

SALMA. Mum!

LEYLA. Cultures are changing now, merging.

LUBLY. Not our culture.

ALEYA. Stay out of it, Leyla.

SHULÉ. Education is a waste of time anyway – you don't need exams or anything these days, you can just go to the Job Centre and get free money.

KOLPHANA. Yes, this country has too much money. It makes people lazy. Especially the women. They want to perform like dancing puppets.

MARIAH. What's wrong with that?

LEYLA. Yeah?

    MARIAH *and* LEYLA *dance a few steps together.*

LUBLY. Stop it!

MARIAH / LEYLA. What?

LUBLY (*to* MARIAH). You know what.

ALEYA. Leyla!

SHULÉ. It is all just showing off to attract men, who are useless anyway.

KOLPHANA. Women should be working at home, supporting their families. Not dancing about on TV.

LEYLA. Why can't we do both?

MARIAH. Yeah.

ALEYA. Well, it's up to other women what they do. But it's not for us.

LEYLA. Mum, we love a good sing-song!

ALEYA. Shush.

SALMA. It wasn't all wasted. I'm a primary schoolteacher now so I teach music and drama.

KOLPHANA. Exactly, it is for babies.

NILUFA. We know you always wanted to act, Salma.

SALMA. Have another grape, Nilufa.

NILUFA. I've had enough grapes!

LUBLY. Bengali women can't act, it's embarrassing.

SALMA. Exactly.

MARIAH. I can act.

HASINA. I can act!

KOLPHANA. No, Mother, you can shout. That's not the same.

LUBLY. Leave acting to the Indians.

KOLPHANA. Yes, let the Indians flaunt themselves.

MARIAH. I want to be an actress!

LUBLY. Subhanallah! Zano shanty nai.

MARIAH. Would you chuck me out?

LUBLY. Mariah, do not start this.

MARIAH. Do you think Dad would?

LUBLY. Would anyone like more chai?

MARIAH. You wouldn't dare. Not again.

LUBLY. That's enough!

LEYLA (*to* ALEYA). What does she mean?

ALEYA. Nothing. Be quiet.

HASINA. Mariah, come and help me with Nilufa's mehndi.

NILUFA. Yes, let's not start this.

LUBLY (*of* MARIAH). She started it!

MARIAH. Why don't you tell them what you did, Mum?

SHULÉ (*to* KOLPHANA). Does she mean what I think she means?

KOLPHANA. Oh yes.

MARIAH. What you and Dad both did.

SALMA. Mariah, stop this right now!

MARIAH. You suffered too, Salma! They might not have kicked you out but they crushed all your spirit.

SALMA. How can you say that?

MARIAH. Because it's true!

HASINA. Mariah, calm yourself. Now is not the time.

NILUFA. Yeah, it's my mehndi.

MARIAH. But I miss her! She should be here and she's not!

LEYLA. Who?

MARIAH. Ripa!

LUBLY throws the pot of chai across the room.

LUBLY. Do not mention her name in this house! Do you understand me? Do! Not! Mention it!

Shocked silence, for some time.

Then, the doorbell goes.

Pause.

HASINA. Maybe I should –

MARIAH. I'll go.

MARIAH exits.

HASINA (*to* LUBLY). Do not punish your daughter for having spirit, Lubly. That is my fault. It is like a force. Impossible to keep inside.

Offstage, MARIAH *screams.*

Everyone freezes.

MARIAH *comes back in with* RIPA.

RIPA *is dripping wet from being in the rain outside.*

Thunder rolls gently underneath the following.

MARIAH. It's Ripa!

RIPA (*to audience*). My name ripples round the room.

NARRATORS (*whisper*). Her name ripples
Ripples ripples
Ripa Ripa.
Round the room
Ssssssh

RIPA. And I know exactly what every single one of em is thinkin.

LUBLY. How dare you come back, today of all days.

NILUFA. Little sister, what have you done?

SALMA. You bring shame coming here.

MARIAH. I am so happy to see you.

SHULÉ. What a brilliant scandal.

KOLPHANA. You filthy little floozy.

HASINA. We're exactly the same.

ALEYA. I've heard all about you.

LEYLA. Wow. She's buff.

RIPA. And I'm soakin
    And shakin
    And tryin a get warm
    But the voices around me
    Like some kinda storm

LUBLY. How dare you –

NILUFA. Little sister –

MARIAH. So happy –

SALMA. Bring shame –

SHULÉ. What scandal –

KOLPHANA. You floozy –

HASINA. Exactly the same –

    This can repeat a couple of times to some sort of build.

RIPA. Stop!

    RIPA *is shivering.*

    Could someone please get me a towel?

    MARIAH *goes to fetch one.*

    She comes back with a towel and a change of clothes.

    During the following speeches, RIPA *takes off her outer
    layer of street clothes and wraps herself in Bengali silks and
    a headscarf.*

    MARIAH, LEYLA *and* HASINA *help her.*

The transformation from modern clothing into traditional dress should be striking.

*During the following speeches, the group splits into two – pro- and anti-*RIPA.

NILUFA *is caught in the middle.*

The others address their following thoughts to the audience.

LUBLY. Ever since she was five, she was a tearaway. The girl is possessed by jinn[13]. She is not my daughter, not my blood, not mine. Some other family had her.

NILUFA. Sis, it's so good to see you. I thought you'd be in prison or something, people have spread such nasty things. But why tonight? Why at my mehndi? This is gonna be so hard.

SALMA. She rejected us, started to change. Hung around with boys, talking in slang. This might be East London but we are respectable.

MARIAH. I loved her so much, she was my role model. Stuck up for me in school when I was getting bullied. Sometimes I'd stay up late and secretly listen to her on the radio.

SHULÉ. She was always listening to her music up loud, every night. All these banging beats and raps. Really fast, like this – (*Does an impression.*) Silly nonsense music. Only people on drugs can listen to that.

KOLPHANA. She was always different, always a weirdo. Listening to this 'grime' music. Grime is dirt! But she chose it over her family. There is no going back on that.

HASINA. It is funny how history repeats. I ran away to follow my heart, she ran away to follow her music. The difference is, I never went back.

ALEYA. I saw pictures of her, she was a beautiful girl. But I heard the gossip too. But I never believe gossip, I prefer to judge for myself.

LEYLA. I heard she used to spit[14] on pirate radio. In Arabic sometimes too! Man, that is so cool, what a wicked fusion.

RIPA. I shouldn't have come.

LUBLY / SALMA / SHULÉ / KOLPHANA. You shouldn't.

MARIAH / HASINA / ALEYA / LEYLA. You should.

The split in the group is complete, with MARIAH, HASINA, LEYLA *and* ALEYA *facing down* LUBLY, SALMA, KOLPHANA *and* SHULÉ.

NILUFA *is caught in the middle and hovers between both sides.*

LUBLY *goes to the phone.*

LUBLY. I'm calling your father.

MARIAH, HASINA, ALEYA *and* LEYLA *move to stop her.*

MARIAH / HASINA / ALEYA / LEYLA. No!

LUBLY. Salma, give me your mobile.

ALEYA. Lubly, please.

LUBLY. Aleya, I am surprised at you. The others I would expect, but you?

ALEYA. I just think we should listen to what your daughter has to say.

LUBLY. She is no daughter of mine.

NILUFA. Mum, please.

LUBLY. I can't breathe when she's around!

NILUFA. I would like to hear what she has to say. It's my night.

LUBLY *considers.*

LUBLY. So be it. (*To* RIPA.) Speak.

RIPA *steps up. She is nervous at first but soon finds her flow.*

RIPA. First up I want to apologise
To Mum, Nilufa and all you guys
I hope you don't think that I'm being unwise
Don't wanna scandalise your mehndi
Want you to know I don't mean to offend you.

NILUFA. Of course not. Please go on.

RIPA. Four years ago we all know what I did
   I selfishly followed my heart not my head
   Defied your advice and went out on my own
   Knowing the price that I'd pay was my home
   I hurt you all bad and it's been a long time
   I know it won't heal with a couple of rhymes.

SALMA. You can say that again.

RIPA. So I wanted a career as a pro MC
   Cos there ain't a Bengali what flows like me
   Took my chances on my own in the music industry
   Swear down, it was hard
   Missed my family bare
   But I paid it no regard
   Pretended like I didn't care
   Grafted and prayed
   Cos Ripa's deep not shallow
   Knowing no one's self-made
   Man, they owe it all to Allah
   Yeah, my faith's for real
   It's as solid as my rhymes
   And if rhyming's unIslamic
   That makes Arabic a crime.

   The others murmur. RIPA *falters.* HASINA *takes her hand.*

HASINA. Go on, child. Truth conquers all things.

RIPA. But I had this debate with Dad four years ago
   Don't want it all again it interrupts my flow
   I'm back here tonight for my sister Nilufa
   I've missed you, big sister
   And this is the proof
   Been struggling now on my own for four years
   I've missed you, I'm tired, my eyes hurt from the tears.

SHULÉ (*to* SALMA). Do you believe her?

SALMA. I don't know, I can't listen.

RIPA. But I'm older and wiser, I realise the cost
   Of throwing this away, of the scale of my loss

Cos what is it in life that keeps us in place?
Like the anchor of a ship – it's community, it's faith.

KOLPHANA. Yes!

RIPA. I've had my bit of fun and now I see my life ahead of me
Turn to face the sun cos now it's time to make a better me
And I ain't gonna get it in the music industry
Cos Britain ain't ready for a Muslim MC.

MARIAH. For real, man.

RIPA. Ain't even gonna tell you what I did to get by
But I lived to tell the tale, I'm here, I survived
Now I want my own mehndi, marriage, feeling connected
Husband, kids, all the things I once rejected.

KOLPHANA. Are you listening to this, Lubly?

RIPA. I wanna grow up, settle down, have a few little me's
Cos when a man supports his wife is when a woman's truly
free
Yeah, let the men do the work, pay the bills, get bored
Cos we've got a job that's really more important
Raising the next generation
Cos if you educate a woman then you educate a nation.

The women murmur their agreement.

Passing on faith and wisdom
Showing there's more than a place in the system.

MARIAH. Word.

NILUFA. What?

RIPA. Yeah, I want my Bengali identity back
Cos without it, I'm nothing, and it's holding me back
Women performing? Yeah, tell me about it
Want my sari and scarf, I'm naked without it
Wearing this, I'm judged for my mind not my looks
My words taken serious, like in some book.

LUBLY *has isolated herself from the group and turned
away.*

RIPA *goes to her.*

(*To* LUBLY.) Mum, all I ever wanted was to feel like your equal
You've had your life, and now I'm the sequel
I know that right now you're feelin the friction
But I want you to know there ain't no contradiction
You've always written me off as a dreamer
But what you're looking at now is a modern Muslima[15].

*The pro-*RIPA *group cheer and clap.*

The room erupts with opinions, only LUBLY *is silent.*

NILUFA. You never cease to amaze me, Ripa. I don't know whether to laugh or cry. Come here. (*Hugs her.*)

SALMA. This is so embarrassing, I can't believe she's doing this to us. (*To* RIPA.) You are so selfish!

MARIAH. Leave her alone! That was wicked, man! Ignore them, ignore them. I have never heard anything like that! That was the nangest[16] fing *ever*.

SHULÉ. I still don't see why she can't talk like a normal human being. Do you think she's on drugs? I think she is, look at her eyes.

KOLPHANA. That is so sweet, she wrote a poem for her mum! Lubly, whatever you think, that is a sweet thing to do. Don't be too harsh on her.

HASINA. Lubly, this is a young woman you can be proud of. Her truth shall set us all free.

ALEYA. Are you okay, sweetheart? Whatever anyone says, that was really brave. If they're angry it's because they're hurting. Okay?

LEYLA. That is so exciting, I ain't never seen a Bengali do that! I'm gonna write about this on my course. Do it again, I wanna film it on my phone!

RIPA (*tearful*). Yeah, man, I'm fine, it's cool. It's all good, it's all good.

LUBLY. Enough!

Everyone falls silent.

Tense pause.

Get this girl out of my house.

MARIAH / LEYLA / ALEYA / HASINA / KOLPHANA / NILUFA (*shouting*). No!

SALMA. Maybe you should go, Ripa.

SHULÉ. Yes, it is not right that you came.

SALMA. What if Dad comes back?

RIPA. Then I'll talk to him.

SHULÉ. Have you written a silly poem for him too?

SALMA. Mind your own business, Shulé.

MARIAH / LEYLA / ALEYA / HASINA / KOLPHANA / NILUFA. Yeah!

SALMA. This isn't your family.

SHULÉ *looks embarrassed and backs down.*

LUBLY. It is *my* family. And I want her to go.

ALEYA *steps forward.*

ALEYA. Lubly, think about this.

LUBLY. I have thought about it for four years!

ALEYA. Just calm down.

LUBLY. I am calm!

ALEYA. Listen to me. If there is one thing I have learned from being a mother it is this: You must allow your children their identity crisis. There is so much for them to carry today. They are Bengali, they are Muslim, they are British, they are East London, they are young, they are women. Is it any wonder they struggle to hold it all? Allow them to drop a few. They will come back for them when the time is right. You just have to wait.

LUBLY. No.

ALEYA. Allow them to celebrate who they are, piece by piece. We are lucky that we are in a country which allows them to do that.

LUBLY. I cannot allow it.

HASINA. Lubly, please. It was different for us. If you keep this up, you may lose her for good.

LUBLY. I have already lost her for good. She is a total disgrace. In all this time, I never missed her.

ALEYA. You don't mean that.

LUBLY. She is just a memory.

ALEYA. Stop this.

LUBLY. I still cherish the baby memories, but she's dead to me now. A baby that died. It is very sad but there is nothing you can do.

NILUFA. Mum, please stop this!

MARIAH. Yeah!

RIPA. I want to come back, Mum. I need to come back.

SALMA. Will you give up all this stupid rapping?

RIPA. I don't know.

SALMA. You can't have everything, Ripa! You can't come back and settle down and be Bengali and still make an idiot of yourself jumping about on stage.

MARIAH. Why not?

SALMA. Because life ain't MTV, Mariah! It's not stupid dreams about bling and gangsters!

RIPA. It ain't about that for me.

SALMA. Life is not a pick 'n' mix!

MARIAH. I know, it's a stupid samosa, innit!

RIPA. I hate samosas!

LUBLY. Then you hate *us*.

Pause. SALMA *comforts* LUBLY. HASINA *comforts* RIPA.

RIPA. No – no, that's not what I'm saying.

NILUFA. Please, everyone, can we stop this?

HASINA. Yes, this is too much.

SALMA. She has to choose, Nilufa.

RIPA. Don't make me.

SALMA. You must.

LUBLY. Yes. It is our world, or theirs. Choose.

RIPA *(tearful)*. Please. Don't do this. You're tearing me in two.
    I'm not like you. I'm not. I'm not.

SALMA. Perhaps you should go, Ripa.

NILUFA / MARIAH. No!

RIPA. What does it matter how anyone lives their life?

LUBLY. It matters when it affects our eejot[17].

SALMA. Yeah.

LUBLY. This family can never get that back. *(To* RIPA.)
    Coming here from Bangladesh, you don't understand. The
    sacrifices made by your father and I. For you. For all of you.
    We wanted the best. And you wanted to become a 'rapper'.
    This is the greatest insult.

    RIPA *steps forward so she is facing* LUBLY, *centre stage.*
    RIPA *puts her hand on her heart.*

RIPA. Then I ask for forgiveness. Inshallah[18].

    LUBLY *just stands and looks at* RIPA.

    Ammā[19]. Please.

HASINA. Lubly, your daughter has made her feelings known
    with her song. Now it is your turn. You must do one of these
    'raps'.

SALMA. Don't be ridiculous, Grandma.

HASINA. She will feel better afterwards.

LUBLY. I just want to be left alone.

RIPA (*upset*). Fine. But I want everyone here to know that I tried. I tried.

RIPA *turns to go*. MARIAH *and* NILUFA *block her exit*.

MARIAH. No!

NILUFA. It's my mehndi and I want you to stay!

MARIAH. Me too!

MARIAH *and* NILUFA *each take one of* RIPA*'s hands*.

LUBLY (*to* RIPA). Ripa, you stay away from Mariah!

RIPA. What?

MARIAH. Why?

LUBLY. I do not want to lose my one remaining daughter.

MARIAH. I ain't going nowhere.

LUBLY. Salma is married, Nilufa is going, Ripa has gone. Mariah, she is the last. Don't you dare take her with you.

RIPA. I'm not.

LUBLY. You are too alike.

MARIAH. Are we? Wicked.

NILUFA. No one's going anywhere, Mum. Look at us. We're here. Back together, complete. Salma?

NILUFA *extends her free hand to* SALMA, *who reluctantly comes over and takes it. All four daughters are now standing in a line holding hands*.

Your girls. All home. After all these years.

LUBLY *is moved by this sight, though she tries not to be*.

HASINA. This is a beautiful thing!

KOLPHANA. I think I'm going to cry.

SHULÉ. Me too.

NILUFA. Let's just enjoy it, Mum. Just for tonight. We can work things out in the morning.

ALEYA. Lubly, I would gently remind you that in Islam one must forgive.

MARIAH. Don't fight it, Mum. I know you want her back. We all do.

LUBLY. But she has tarnished us. She has tarnished you – your reputations, your chances of getting married.

MARIAH. So?

NILUFA. Ssh.

LUBLY. No one will want to let their son into this family.

ALEYA. This is not true. You are still good enough for me, and for my son. God has given you a second chance with your daughter, Lubly. You may be losing Nilufa tomorrow, but you are gaining Ripa tonight. This is God's hand at work, providing balance. It is God's will that your daughter came back tonight. You must forgive. Especially when it has been asked from the heart.

RIPA. Mum?

LUBLY. My other daughters must forgive her too.

NILUFA. I forgive her.

MARIAH. I forgive her.

HASINA. So do I.

LEYLA. I forgive her too!

ALEYA. Leyla, shush.

LEYLA. Why? I'm almost her daughter now.

KOLPHANA. We must all forgive, Aleya is right. It is a sin not to.

SHULÉ. I forgive her.

KOLPHANA (*to* SHULÉ). Good. I forgive you too.

LUBLY. Salma? What about you?

MARIAH. She's married already, it doesn't matter.

SALMA. I… I don't know.

NILUFA. Please, Salma. It's the best mehndi present you could give me.

SALMA. Dad would never forgive.

MARIAH. But you're not Dad.

RIPA. Salma. Please. For Nilufa.

NILUFA. For Mum.

MARIAH. For yourself, Salma.

> SALMA *hesitates then awkwardly offers her hand.* RIPA *ignores it and embraces her instead. There are a few gasps.*

> SALMA *pulls away from the embrace and hides her face.* KOLPHANA *and* SHULÉ *offer her tissues.*

> RIPA *faces* LUBLY.

RIPA. Mum?

> *Tense pause.*

ALEYA (*to* LUBLY). You have such a brave daughter. You should be proud.

> ALEYA *puts her arm round* LEYLA.

She is your baby. She will always be your baby.

> RIPA *goes to* LUBLY *and they embrace.*

ALL (*whispers*). Oh my God
   Look at that
   That's amazing
   Alhumdulillah[20]
   I never thought I'd see it
   I can't watch
   Does this mean everything's alright?
   It's a start.

> LUBLY *breaks away from the embrace to hide her tears.*

KOLPHANA *and* SHULÉ *offer tissues.*

SALMA. What are we going to do about Dad?

HASINA. I will speak to him!

KOLPHANA. No, leave him to me.

LUBLY. No. I will speak to him.

RIPA. What?

NILUFA. Really?

MARIAH. Serious?

LUBLY. Yes. I cannot promise. Four years is a long time. It may take four more. But I will try, as you have tried tonight. Aleya is right. You have set an example, Ripa, and I will do my best to follow.

RIPA. Thank you.

LUBLY *and* RIPA *embrace again.*

MARIAH. I'm scared. Scared about Dad.

HASINA *takes* KOLPHANA*'s arm.*

HASINA. Nonsense!

KOLPHANA. Yes, relax.

HASINA. He is no match for the women in his life.

KOLPHANA. Your father comes later.

HASINA. Yes, this is *our* time. This is our night. Mehndi night.

Music starts, and singing.

As the cast go through their dance moves, they start to un-mould themselves from their characters and return to themselves.

NARRATORS. And there we've got to leave it
A happy but sad sort of ending
A bit like life though, innit
I spose
But if there's one thing we've learned

It's that every ending
Is also a beginning
Like when you walk on out of here now
You'll take a little piece of us with you somehow
Cos bonds between people are made for repairing
And lives, like samosas
Are made for sharing
So thank you for sharing your lives with our show
Khoda Hafez[21]
Mind how you go.

The End.

1. 'Scottish' due to the premiere of this play taking place at the Edinburgh Fringe Festival. The line can be changed or cut if the play is performed elsewhere

2. A Bengali sweet

3. Hello, 'Peace be upon you' – Arabic

4. Traditional Bengali folk songs

5. 'Oh God!' – Arabic

6. 'There is no peace in my life!' – Sylheti

7. A term of respect for an elder woman

8. Hanging out, chilling – East London slang

9. 'Do you understand?' – Sylheti

10. Traditional Bengali proverb

11. Forbidden – Arabic

12. A mild stimulant which is chewed, a bit like chewing tobacco, widespread in South Asia

13. Spirit being, a widespread belief among Muslims

14. 'Rap' – East London slang

15. Female Muslim

16. Good, great – East London slang

17. Honour, reputation, respect – Sylheti

18. 'God willing' – Arabic

19. 'Mum' – Sylheti

20. 'Praise be to God' – Arabic

21. Goodbye, farewell – Sylheti

STOLEN SECRETS

Author's Note

Stolen Secrets was the second play Mulberry Theatre Company presented at the Edinburgh Festival. It was a deliberate decision not to write another overtly 'Asian play' after *Mehndi Night*. Instead, we used a direct-address ensemble storytelling style to place the cast as narrators on the stage action – thereby freeing them up from the naturalistic necessity of having to play characters who look like themselves. In this way, a group of mostly Asian, teenage girls were able to play cocky young men, elderly white women, policemen, fathers and brothers. This presented a healthy challenge for the production team, and began to develop an aesthetic for the fledgling Mulberry Theatre Company. It was also the first time we offered 'arts apprenticeships', shadowing professionals in stage management and theatre design, something we now offer on every production.

The darker emotional truths of *Stolen Secrets* – though heavily fictionalised – were originally from seeds 'harvested' from within the school. Our designer that year built us a set of special 'Secrets Boxes', to which students, artists and staff were invited to make anonymous contributions. The boxes were opened in rehearsals and the contents used as the starting point for improvisations.

The neutral ensemble of storytellers gives this play a wide appeal for other performance groups. The only rule of thumb is that, generally, each new line in the ensemble sections (i.e. with no character name attached) indicates a new speaker. In this way, the narrators' lines could be distributed between two actors or twenty, or anything in between. The 'secrets' can also be performed individually or omitting one or two, allowing different running times but without greatly affecting the overall narrative. (However, if two or more secrets are to be performed together I would recommend retaining the Intro and Outro for use as a framing device.)

Once again, I owe a debt to my co-tutors on this project, Julia
Voce and Camille Cettina, as well as our designer Kollodi
Norton, who rose so boldly to the challenges of this new style.
Under their tutelage, the young cast developed an extraordinary
physical storytelling aesthetic which beautifully complemented
the lyricism of the text.

Stolen Secrets was first performed on 11 August 2008 at Venue
45, Edinburgh, with the following ensemble:

Parvin Akhtar
Nabilah Begum
Rabia Begum
Kim Hashi
Sultana Islam
Munirun Nessa
Yasmin Sadek
Fahmida Siddika

Directors	Julia Voce and Camille Cettina
Designer	Kollodi Norton
Stage Management Apprentice	Aysha Begum
Design Apprentice	Bushra Khatun
Catering Support	Shara Banu

48

Characters

INTRO
NARRATORS

PILLOW FIGHT
NARRATORS

MAKE 'N' MEND
NARRATORS
MOTHER
DAUGHTER
BOY

MRS JONES
NARRATORS
SARA
MUM
POLICEMAN 1
POLICEMAN 2
MRS JONES

NOT A GIRL
NARRATORS
NASIMA / NASIM
MUM
DAD
SHOREDITCH GIRLS
DRUNK

MY SILENT SISTER
NARRATORS

OUTRO
NARRATORS

Intro

A montage of whispered secrets.

Recorded:

When my mum finally died, I said 'thank you'
Automatic doors make me feel special
I touched this guy's bum on the bus
I'm scared to laugh in case I piss
I am a descendant of the Ancient Egyptians
I have a split personality
I saw a dead body
I feel sorry for atheists
I steal things off the back of lorries
I'm scared of teddy bears
When someone hurts me mentally I hurt myself physically
I feel like my family hold me hostage in my own house
I'm having an affair with a married man
I found a lump on my breast and haven't told anyone
I'm Muslim, he's Catholic
I spit in my uncle's tea
I pretend to be someone else online
I have dreams about all the streets disappearing
I'm scared of the red button on our TV
I killed my brother's pet hamster
The doctors say my mum is going to die
I'm scared of almost everything
My cousin's gay
I fantasise about killing my sisters

Live:

Secretsssssss
Shhhhhhhhhhhhhhhh
Sad secrets
Silly secrets
Sorry secrets
Shameful secrets
Shocking
Sinful
Silent
True
Hidden
Private
Screened from view
They live in the heart
But swim in the brain
Tiny, but sharp
Like darts of pain

Secrets shouldn't be confused with lies
Or gossip
Or silly rumours
Those things are nasty
Like little tumours
Secrets are real
Secrets are true
Sharp like a razor
They'll cut you in two

Top secret
Like government files
Leak it
And you'll meet it at night in your dreams
Speak it
And it'll build like a deafening scream

You gotta conceal it
The secret
Bury it in cold deep earth
Or fling it in the sea
Lock it in your heart of hearts
And throw away the key

You can try all this
Do your best
But sometimes
Sometimes
You get up in the morning
After a restless night
Check the box
Sealed tight
Lock blocked up with glue
And it isn't there
It's gone
It's flown
It's stolen away from you

East London
Our ends
Is built on secrets
Ancient secrets
Teenage secrets
Foreign secrets
Wartime secrets
They hide in tower-block stairwells
Under stains on the carpet
In hoods
Gutters
Drops of rain
Between lines of faded newsprint
Or trickling out the drains
Sometimes the whispering gets so loud
It hangs there like a thundercloud.

The sound of distant thunder.

Wanna hear the first one?
Alright, but you gotta promise this goes no further…

Pillow Fight

There's a tower block just near our school
With a broken lift and faded walls.
On the highest floor, scraping the clouds
A family of nine live upside down.
Crammed into a flat that's meant for two
The daughters spill outside onto the roof.
Because the lift has never been repaired,
They can't be bothered going down the stairs,
So out here on the roof is where they go,
The veins of London throbbing far below.
This is the place they play, and eat, and dream,
But in families nothing's ever as it seems.

Seven sisters all alike in looks,
But one likes clothes and one prefers her books,
One's religious, one likes R'n'B,
One likes skiving school till half past three.
One likes babies and wants to be a mum,
Another's clever but pretends she's dumb.
But the youngest is the one that holds the secret
If we tell you what it is you'd better keep it.

First thing in the morning once it's light,
And also before bed last thing at night,
All seven sisters head up to the roof
And like to have this massive pillow fight.
Whack! In the back as London wakes
Whack! In the face as the sunrise breaks
Whack! In the head as the moonlight shines
Whack! As the youngest loses her mind.

Cos all she can think of is how much they hurt her
Her head boiling over with thoughts of murder
Her pillow goes from white to red
As each of her sisters falls down dead.

'I hate you, I hate you, I hate you!' She screams
And can no longer tell what's real or a dream
Rocks fill her pillow
As hate fills her heart
Imagining ripping her sisters apart
Taking their bodies, and in one single throw
Watching them fall to the tarmac below.

At the end she is crying and no one knows why
She clutches her pillow and looks at the sky
Sends up a question to the heavens above
Asking God why she hates those she should love.

But God never answers her strange little prayer
So they gather their pillows and go back downstairs.

Make 'n' Mend

NARRATORS. Turn right down Pedley Street
Past the boarded-up Shoreditch Tube
Past the weeds
And the litter
Raked up like a snowdrift against the disused railway tracks
Watch as the terraces seem to get smaller
Is it your imagination?
Or a trick of the light?
Keep walking
Don't be scared
Cos down there's our next secret.

Soon you'll come to a little cul-de-sac
Can't go no further
This is it
Weaver Street
Where the houses are so small
It's like they was built for... I dunno
Oompa-Loompas
Yeah!
Pixies
Or something not quite human.

Anyway, down there
At the far end of Weaver Street
Where you can't go no further
There's a little shop
Make 'n' Mend
The K is like a pair of scissors
And the Ms are made of needles
On the blue-and-white sign above the door.

They open the door.

Go on
In you go

We'll wait out here for you
They know our faces, innit
They know we know their secret.

Inside the shop, MOTHER *and* DAUGHTER *sit repairing a
pile of clothes with a needle and thread.*

Inside, it is so small
A low-flying ceiling
And walls that come up to your face like they want a fight
It's dark
And musty
The smell of second-hand clothes
Stagnant lives
And withered dreams
Like fruit left to rot on the tree.

MOTHER. I want that pile finished by the time we close.
Understand?

DAUGHTER. Yes, Mum.

NARRATORS. But only a hundred yards away
The delights of Brick Lane
Roasting meat
Shisha pipes
The tinkle of laughter
And the sweet scent of freedom
Waft across the summer air
And tug at the Daughter's heart.

DAUGHTER. Mum?

MOTHER. What?

DAUGHTER. If I finish early –

MOTHER. You won't.

DAUGHTER. But if I do –

MOTHER. The answer's no. Get on with your work.

NARRATORS. Of course, what the daughter really wants to say
is:

DAUGHTER. You know what my greatest fear is? Turning into a lonely, bitter, ugly old woman. Just. Like. YOU!

NARRATORS. The ball of longing inside her
    Wants to grab her mother and shout:

DAUGHTER. I am not your prisoner! Not your slave!

NARRATORS. But of course she never does
    Instead, she dreams
    Dreams of the boy who will come to whisk her away
    Tall
    Dark
    Spiky hair
    Chiselled jaw
    Romantic stare
    Early twenties
    Or even late teens
    Decent car
    Moschino jeans.

MOTHER. What are you daydreaming about?

DAUGHTER. Nothing.

MOTHER. Less shirking, more working.

DAUGHTER. Yes, Mum.

MOTHER. Gormless child.

NARRATORS. Then one day like God was listening
    With rain outside and tarmac glistening
    Through the puddles struts this guy
    And her heart becomes a butterfly
    He goes past the weeds and the railway tracks
    And right to the end of the cul-de-sac
    Then opens the door and into the shop
    And her heart is bangin like it ain't gonna stop
    Burstin at the seams
    Unravelling like loose thread
    Heaving
    Hurting
    And she *wishes* she'd said:

DAUGHTER. Oh my God! You are so BUFF!

NARRATORS. But this poor girl's just too uptight

Instead she nods and goes:

DAUGHTER. Alright.

BOY. Alright. I got this shirt, innit. Pocket come off in a fight. Can you fix it?

NARRATORS. But she can't even speak
Can't hardly move
Just gives him his slip
And watches him go.

MOTHER. Who was that?

DAUGHTER. Just some guy.

MOTHER. A regular?

DAUGHTER. No.

MOTHER. Hm. New business. Good. Nice shirt. Quality.

DAUGHTER. The pocket's come off.

MOTHER. A five-minute job. Get to it.

NARRATORS. And she does
Though she makes it last
Each stitch like a loving stroke
Binding her heart to his
A cotton pocket to hold her dreams.

And how she dreams
About him fighting
Face hardened
Fists clenched
Blows raining down on his rival
Two boys, locked into battle
Fighting over HER.

He'd win of course
Easily
Then tomorrow
Tomorrow

    Tomorrow
    He'll come back in
    And tell her the news
    He'd won
    And *she* was his prize
    He was here to claim her.

DAUGHTER. We'll fly to America and get married and live in this massive apartment overlooking Central Park and eat hotdogs and ice creams on horse-drawn carriages and kiss on park benches as the sun goes down and Mum would never ever know where I'd gone!

MOTHER. What are you daydreaming about?

DAUGHTER. Nothing.

NARRATORS. Except it wasn't how she dreamed at all
    Instead, he came back in.

BOY. Alright.

DAUGHTER. Alright.

NARRATORS. And though the shirt was ready
    Her heart screamed at the thought of never seeing him again
    And it made her tell a lie:

DAUGHTER. Ain't ready yet.

BOY. Oh.

DAUGHTER. Sorry.

BOY. S'alright.

DAUGHTER. Tomorrow, innit.

BOY. Seen.

NARRATORS. And that was that
    Barely ten words exchanged
    But those words echoed round her heart all night.

DAUGHTER. 'S'alright.' 'Seen.' 'S'alright.' 'Seen.' He must've *seen* that I'm *alright*. And he's coming back for me. Tomorrow!

NARRATORS. And she takes his shirt
   Imagines him in it
   Holding her
   Dancing with her
   Spinning her round in a New York sunset
   Hearts on fire
   Hands on his back
   Breathing him in
   Dancing her away from here
   Away from the weeds and the litter and the railway tracks
   And the too-small house
   And the cul-de-sac.

MOTHER. WHAT ARE YOU DOING?!

DAUGHTER. Nothing!

MOTHER. Give that to me!

> MOTHER *tries to grab the shirt.* DAUGHTER *hangs onto it.*
>
> *They struggle.*

DAUGHTER. No!

MOTHER. I knew there was something going on!

DAUGHTER. Stop it!

MOTHER. You stupid little girl! Do you really think a boy like that would even notice a girl like you?

> *In the struggle the pocket gets torn off the shirt again.*

DAUGHTER. No!

MOTHER. Now look what you've done.

> MOTHER *takes the shirt.*
>
> DAUGHTER *takes the pocket and clutches it to her.*

Give that to me.

> DAUGHTER *cries and shakes her head.*

I won't ask you again.

DAUGHTER *stuffs the pocket into her mouth.*

MOTHER *slaps* DAUGHTER.

Stupid child! Where did I go wrong with you?! You will stay in here, and you will get on with your work until I say you can come out.

MOTHER *locks* DAUGHTER *into the back room.*

DAUGHTER *takes the pocket out of her mouth.*

She takes out a needle to begin work on the huge pile of clothes.

NARRATORS. And that was that
Or so we thought
Locked into the back room for the whole of the next day
So that when the boy came back, it was Mum on the front counter
And the girl was nowhere to be seen.

MOTHER. It was not possible to save the pocket. I am sorry.
You may have a discount.

NARRATORS. And he paid
And he went
But then
Then
Then
Mum went into the back room
To tell her daughter it was over
But oh my God
What she found there
No word of a lie
What she saw will stay with her till the day that she dies.

Her daughter had taken a needle and thread
And sewn the boy's pocket to her own naked flesh
Each stitch like a loving stroke
Through the soft skin and down to the bone
The blood flowed thick as she held in her screams
As thick as the pocket that held in her dreams
A permanent seal to sew up her heart
So no other man could tear it apart.

Mum held her down as she cleaned up the wound
Unpicked the stitches by the light of the moon
Held back the tears with practised control
And breathed not a word to one single soul.

Make
Make
Make
And mend.

Mrs Jones

NARRATORS. A bit further east, yeah, down past the gasworks
   Where the A1205 hacks its way
   Like a traffic-jam boundary between Tower Hamlets and
   Newham
   You've got Mile End Park
   Long
   Thin
   Running north to south
   Like a green sticking plaster on an old old wound.

   See them flats backing onto it?
   Nice view
   Yeah
   Well there's a girl in there had a pretty weird experience
   Oh yeeeeah, I like this one
   It's sad, man
   Shut up, you'll give it away.

   There was this old lady lived on the ground floor
   Mum said her name was Mrs Jones
   But Sara and her friends used to call her the Witch
   Cos she had this long hooked nose
   With warts all down it
   Eurgh
   And she'd sit in her flat all day
   With the curtains drawn
   Just her and her black cat
   (We made the cat up, but she probably had one)
   Yeah, she probably made potions
   And cast spells on all the neighbours
   Stop it, you're giving me shivers
   Anyway, one day, yeah, there was some building works
   going on
   Outside the block
   New sewers or cable TV or something like that

When all of a sudden there was this clang
As the digger hit something
Big
Solid
Metal
Buried deep
Like a secret
Or a memory of another time.

POLICEMEN 1 *and* 2 *knock on a door.* SARA *answers it.*

POLICEMAN 1. I'm sorry to bother you, my love, but we're evacuating the building.

SARA. Why?

POLICEMAN 2. There's been a bomb discovered in your back-yard. If you wouldn't mind leaving the premises?

SARA. Mum! Bomb!

MUM *appears.*

MUM. Oh, not again.

NARRATORS. Happens around here all the time, dunnit
Cos of the war.

Downstairs it was chaos
People everywhere
Blue lights and sirens
Plastic tape and radios
Army trucks all fully loaded
Anyone'd think the thing had already exploded.

The police, mind you, were lovin it.

POLICEMAN 1. This way, please!

POLICEMAN 2. Don't stop for a gossip, ladies, it might be the last one you ever have.

POLICEMAN 1. Bomb in the area!

POLICEMAN 2. It might be old but it's still dangerous!

POLICEMAN 1. Bit like some of you!

POLICEMAN 1 / 2. Hahahahaha!

NARRATORS. And everyone was laughing
    And smiling
    And drinkin sweet tea
    The café was givin it away for free
    And it was like that thing you sometimes hear about
    East London at its finest
    The Spirit of the Blitz
    Had somehow slipped out of its grave
    Out of that hole in our backyard
    And wrapped itself around us all
    Warm
    Friendly
    And kind.

    MUM *goes over to one of the* POLICEMEN.

MUM. Excuse me. Did you check on Mrs Jones in Flat 1? She
    lives there on her own.

POLICEMAN. Nah, flat's empty, love.

NARRATORS. But chaos is an open door for mischief
    And Sara had mischief in her soul
    And nosiness on her mind
    So when no one was looking
    She stole back in
    To see what she could find.

    Last time they were evacuated
    She snooped around Flat 2
    And Oh My God you'll never guess what she found –
    But this is about Flat 1
    Yeah.

    Back in the block it was quiet
    Echoey
    Echoey
    Echoey
    Stop it, this is serious
    She snuck up to Flat 1
    And slowly creaked open the door

This was her chance to finally find out what witchy things
Mrs Jones was up to in there.

Inside it was still
Like the air hadn't moved for years
Memories hanging heavy like old fag smoke
Yellow
Like faded lives.

She was surprised
It actually looked like quite a normal living room.

SARA. Mrs Jones?

NARRATORS. No sign of a cauldron
    Or any bats or cats
    Just a battered sofa covered in biscuit crumbs
    A knackered old telly
    And a set of ducks on the wall.

SARA. Mrs Jones?

NARRATORS. She checked the kitchen
    No pumpkins
    No voodoo dolls
    No magic charms
    Not even a broomstick
    Just a lukewarm kettle on the stove
    And a half-eaten microwave meal in the sink.

SARA. Mrs Jones?

NARRATORS. She checked the bathroom
    Though what a witch's bathroom would look like she didn't
    really know
    This one had pink loo roll
    A fluffy toilet-seat lid
    And one of those contraptions to help you out of the bath.

SARA. Mrs Jones?

NARRATORS. Then finally she checked the tiny old bedroom
    Peeling wallpaper
    And yes! Cobwebs!
    But nothing else

Not even a pointy hat
Just an unmade bed
And a weirdly massive wardrobe the size of a phone box.

SARA. Mrs Jones?

NARRATORS. Then
A tiny noise
Short
High-pitched
Like opening a can of Coke
Psht!
Man, I swear that was a sneeze!
Comin from the wardrobe!

SARA. Mrs Jones!

NARRATORS. And there she was
Clinging to the blouses and pleated skirts
Not cackling
Not evil
Just scared
Mrs Jones like a bag of bones.

MRS JONES. Why are you in my house?

NARRATORS. And Sara felt suddenly ashamed.

SARA. Th-th-th-there's a bomb outside. You have to leave.
Hang on. What are you doing in the wardrobe?

NARRATORS. And Mrs Jones told her.

MRS JONES. You young uns don't know what it's like
To be alone every single night
For sixty years it's been the same
And every year I thought the pain
Would ease. But it doesn't.
My David died in '45
Shot down in some foreign sky
And since then I've had only this
A private war of loneliness.
This wardrobe was his
It still has his smell

In here it's like he's holding me
A piece of heaven in the midst of hell.
Please, leave me be. Won't do any harm.
Let this bomb take me back to my David's arms.

SARA. We – we thought you were a witch.

NARRATORS. And as soon as the words were out of her mouth
Sara felt the hot flush of regret.

MRS JONES. No. I'm Mrs Jones. Now please leave me be.

NARRATORS. And as she closed the wardrobe door
A splinter of Mrs Jones's pain lodged itself in Sara's heart.

Soon the police said the bomb team had made it safe
Took the bomb on a truck to some secret place
Sixty years in the ground had caused this corrosion
So there weren't gonna be no massive explosion
So they went back inside and Mum put on the kettle
But Sara was finding it harder to settle
Just thinking about being lonely
Cold
And old.

Then later that night came a tap at the door
Tiny really, like three drops of rain
And there was Mrs Jones, with her walking frame
She'd struggled alone up the stairs just to say.

MRS JONES. This is our secret, let's keep it that way.

SARA. And handed me a tin of mushy green peas.
I said: 'Don't worry. It's safe with me.'

NARRATORS. From that day on
When Sara's friends would laugh at the lady in Flat 1
Who sat at home in the dark all day
And call her a witch or an evil old crone
Sara would always stop them and say:

SARA. No, she isn't. Her name's Mrs Jones.

Not a Girl

NARRATORS. There's this girl lives down Limehouse way
Near where the canal meets Bartlett Park
Nasima
Nice enough
So long as you stay on her good side
This girl can handle herself, innit.

NASIMA. What you sayin?

NARRATORS. Nuttin
Chill, man
There's boys scared of this chick, narmsayin[1].

NASIMA. What you chattin?

NARRATORS. Allow it, man.

She's nineteen, yeah
So a year out of college
But unemployed the whole time
But not cos she ain't clever or nuttin
No way, this girl is smart
Wanted to go university
But to study Engineering
And that's where it all fell apart.

MUM. Why can't you study teaching or nursing like a normal girl?

NASIMA. I am normal. I just wanna do engineering, innit.

DAD. No daughter of mine will be doing this.

NASIMA. Why not?

DAD. I will not pay for such a perversion!

NASIMA. Why not?

MUM. Are you a boy or a girl?

NASIMA. Girl, I spose.

DAD. Well start acting like it then!

NARRATORS. Nasima's always been a tomboy, yeah
Everyone always says it
And she feels it herself.

NASIMA *is sorting through some dresses and saris.*

NASIMA. Yuk. Yuk. Eurgh. No way. Gimme jeans and trainers
any day.

NARRATORS. So that's what she wears
All through college anyway
Then sometimes her mum would say:

MUM. Nasima! How will you ever get a husband dressed like
that?

NASIMA. Maybe I don't want a husband.

MUM. Nonsense! Every girl wants a husband.

NASIMA. Well, maybe I ain't a girl!

NARRATORS. Only she doesn't say that last bit
Not out loud anyway
But every time a gang of boys go strutting up the road
The longing in her heart makes her think she might
explode.

NASIMA (*to herself*). I'm not a girl. Not a girl. Not. A girl.

NARRATORS. Sometimes
When everyone's out
She sneaks into her brother's room
And tries on his clothes
It started with his baseball cap
She looked good.

NASIMA. Innit.

NARRATORS. Then she slipped on a shirt
Even better.

NASIMA. I know.

NARRATORS. Then she got scared in case anyone noticed
    Put it all back in a hurry.

NASIMA. I can't explain it. I just feel wrong. Nasima is wrong.
    D'ya get me?

NARRATORS. So she started to collect her own secret wardrobe
    Some of it was her brother's
    The odd pair of socks or bit of bling.

BROTHER. Naz, have you seen my gold chain?

NASIMA. Nah, sorry bro.

NARRATORS. Some of it was lost property she'd find on the
    train
    A man's pair of gloves
    Or a Ben Sherman scarf.

NASIMA. Lookin bless.

NARRATORS. Some of it was from charity shops
    T-shirts
    Trainers
    Jackets.

NASIMA. Lookin big.

NARRATORS. Then one night
    She realised she had the lot
    A full outfit
    So
    Quietly
    Stealthily
    Secretly
    She locked her bedroom door and tried it all on
    Flattened her chest with a tight-fitting vest
    And hid her hair under a cap
    Holding her breath as she put on the rest
    Her nerves about ready to snap

    Then, when it was done, she finally allowed herself to look
    in the mirror.

NASIMA. Woah!

NARRATORS. This was different
    This was real
    This was her.

NASIMA. Him!

NARRATORS. Yeah, I spose.

NASIMA. Nasim.

NARRATORS. So she practised the walk.

    NASIMA *walks up and down like a boy*.

    Bigger swagger
    Purse your lips
    Everything's gotta be slower
    More shoulders
    Less hips
    Trousers a little lower.

NASIMA. A'ight, man, I'm doing my best, innit!

NARRATORS. Then, she practised the voice.

NASIMA. Swear down, man.

NARRATORS. Deeper.

NASIMA. Swear down, man.

NARRATORS. Better.

NASIMA. You wanna step to me?

NARRATORS. Harder.

NASIMA. You wanna step to me?

NARRATORS. Harder!

NASIMA. Yo, you wanna step to me? Finkin you a bad man?
    Are you dizzy? You stepped to da wrong bredrin today!
    Dat's how tings are now. I'm da baddest Bengi[2] in dis hood
    now. Me! Nasim! No one else!

NARRATORS. Alright!
    That's what we're talking about!
    And like *that* – Nasim was born!

Ain't no way he was gonna sleep tonight
So he opened her window
And nimble as a cat
A tomcat that is
Dropped down to the street below.

But what now?

NASIMA. Gotta do suttin. Use this. See the world.

NARRATORS. It was then he noticed Dad's minicab
Parked up outside the house
And could that be – ?

NASIMA. No way! The key's still in the ignition!

NARRATORS. Unlocking the door
Seat still warm
And on the horizon a gathering storm
Adjusted the mirror
Adjusted the seat
Made sure his smaller feet could reach
Put on some music
Something suitably hectic
Checked the baseball bat was where Dad kept it.

NASIMA *takes a baseball bat from under the seat*.

NASIMA. Wicked.

NARRATORS. Then turned the key
And held on tight
And started driving through the night.

First fare was an old boy coming out of the pub after last orders
Barely able to slur out a street name.

NASIMA. Fiver, mate. Easy money, innit.

Next was some Shoreditch party girls out on the town
Couldn't be bothered walking from one nightclub to the next.

SHOREDITCH GIRLS. We are fa-mi-ly! I got all my sisters with me!

NASIMA. Tenner please, ladies.

NARRATORS. Couple of hours later he was fifty quid up.

NASIMA. Man, this boy ting is easy. Don't have to look nice.
  Don't hardly have to speak. Just sit there and frown. It was
  made for me.

NARRATORS. So he stopped off at a twenty-four-hour
  Buy some ciggies.

NASIMA. Complete the look, innit, all boys smoke.

NARRATORS. Struttin up to the counter
  Past the queue of drunks
  Clinging for dear life to a samosa or a can of Coke.

NASIMA. Ten Marlboros, cheers, mate.

NARRATORS. But under the strip lights
  The harsh reality of an East London 2 a.m.
  The gaps in her disguise began to show.

DRUNK. Oi, ladyboy!

NARRATORS. Ignore it, Naz, just get out of here.

DRUNK. I said Oi!

NARRATORS. Buy the fags and go!
  Good
  Now walk to the car
  Keep walking
  Nice and slow.

DRUNK. Hey, freak! You deaf?

NARRATORS. Ignore it.

DRUNK. Are you a boy or a girl? It's hard to tell.

NARRATORS. Ignore it, Naz.

NASIMA. No, you know what? A boy wouldn't ignore it, so
  neither will I.

NARRATORS. Naz, no!

NASIMA. Yo, who you callin a girl, big man?

DRUNK. I'm talking to you, boy-girl-man ting.

NARRATORS. Naz, leave it!

DRUNK. Give us a kiss then.

NASIMA. Man, you're sick.

DRUNK. You're the freak.

NARRATORS. Walk away!

DRUNK. Woah, you drivin a cab?

NASIMA. So what if I am?

DRUNK. Check dis one out, boys!

NASIMA. Get away from me.

DRUNK. It's a kiss, or your takings. Choose.

NASIMA. Yeah? I choose this.

NARRATORS. And without hardly thinking
    She's opening up the door
    Diving under the seat
    Grabbing it from the floor.

    NASIMA *takes out the baseball bat.*

    Bam! One to the leg and he's down
    Bam! Back of the head on crown
    Bam! One to small of the back
    Bam! One to the cheek with a crack.

    And it's like all of the pain and all of the rage
    The frustration of years being stuck in the cage
    Of being a girl, not seeing the world
    Has suddenly found its stage.

NASIMA. Yo, you wanna step to me? Finkin you a bad man?
    Are you dizzy? You stepped to da wrong bredrin today!
    Dat's how tings are now. I'm da baddest Bengi in dis hood
    now. Me! Nasim! No one else!

NARRATORS. Standing
    Shaking

Out of breath
Blood on the bat
The echo of death
Then back in the car
Driving she don't even know where
Heart pounding
Tears streaming
Brain screaming.

NASIMA. I'm not a girl! Not a girl! Not! A girl!

NARRATORS. Back at the house
Parks up in the gloom
Back through the window
And into her room
The clothes come off
And with them her dreams
Of being a boy
Of being Nasim
Looking at the flecks of blood with a shudder
Then into her nightie and under the covers.

Next day, from round the way
Police come knocking at the door
Someone got Dad's number plate, outside the all-night shop
Nearly beat some man to death, nearly didn't stop.

And Nasima in her nightie
Is sliding down her bedroom door
Doubled up with pain and guilt
Trembling on the floor.

NASIMA. Dad... Dad... No... No...

NARRATORS. Mum crying in the hall
Brother shouting and punching the wall
Dad staying calm as he's taken away
Nasima upstairs doesn't know what to say.

Tell them
Don't
Tell them
Don't.

So what did she do? We never found out
Just kept the door locked and didn't go out
The secret inside burning like a hot coal
For a secret like that, could burn up your soul.

Not a girl
Not a girl
Not
A girl.

My Silent Sister

My sister was born unable to speak
Something went wrong, we assume
She came out too small, all scrawny and weak
So at home she got her own room.

Me and the others had to sleep in the hall
Or the kitchen or bathroom upstairs
We didn't sleep much so we played up in school
But Mum didn't seem to care.

As my sister got older we'd try to include her
In the games that we'd all go and play
Mum said she was special and not to exclude her
But she mostly just got in the way.

We'd run and we'd scream and we'd laugh and we'd shout
We'd key all the cars and we'd leg it about
We'd rob dinner money by threatening violence
But our sister'd sit there in silence.

Then one day this boy in Year 10 come over
And asked if I'd get him a plaster
He'd grazed up his leg playing football he said
And my heart beat a little bit faster.

So I went to the nurse and got what he asked
And my legs went a little bit weak
Cos back at the playground he put on the plaster
Then gave me a peck on the cheek.

I told all of this to my sister, the eldest
But she laughed and just gave me a shove
Said 'Oh my God I can't wait to tell this!
My little sis is in love!'

And before long the whole school was laughing at me
Including the boy from Year 10
I couldn't believe it – the sister I trusted!
I swore never to trust her again.

After that day things were never the same
I'd never let no one persuade me
To tell them my secrets, instead I'd just keep it
I was too scared in case they betrayed me.

But as you get older the secrets amass
Like a weight that you have to confide
They press at your heart like a seething morass
And it's harder to keep them inside.

The boys that you like, the things that you've tried,
The places you've been, the times that you've lied,
Forbidden but fun, all the rules that you've broken,
The things that you've done that have never been spoken.

They pound in your head, marking time like a bell
And build up till your heart is encrusted
They have to come out but who can you tell
When your favourite sister's not trusted?

It was then that our youngest came into her own
Cos of course! She'd never let slip!
Talking to her is like being alone
A totally one-sided friendship.

And once I knew that, I never looked back
I'd just whisper my secrets all day
Some made her smile, some took her aback
While some made her blood drain away.

Secrets too dark to tell anyone else
Secrets so foul they're infested
Secrets so toxic they're bad for your health
Secrets to get me arrested.

But you know what I loved about telling her stuff?
It was the way that she'd smile and nudge me
Not only was everything safe with her
But she'd listen and not ever judge me.

Then one day my mother announced to us all
That there was this new operation
The doctors could open up our sister's skull
And make a small laceration.

And then they'd insert some gadget or other
Which'd sit inside her brain
And do something complicated and clever
Which'd mean she could speak again!

Imagine my horror as the family sat round
And smiled at this wonderful news
I sat there in silence and looked at the ground
Brain fizzing like a blown fuse.

She'd tell all my secrets! She'd spread all my dirt!
She'd dump me in truckloads of trouble!
She'd get me arrested! She'd get me hurt!
My life would collapse into rubble!

Once they'd all gone I paced up and down
And she smiled and showed me her brace
But all I could do was mutter and frown –
I wanted that smile off her face.

So I went in the kitchen and picked up some scissors
The biggest and sharpest ones
Then went back in the lounge and held her head down
And with one hand I yanked out her tongue.

I took quite a while to cut the tongue off
It was gristly and quite hard to hold
She struggled of course, and clenched up her jaws
But I had all the time in the world.

When it was done, I held up the tongue
It looked like an overripe fig
Or maybe a plum, all covered in scum,
You know tongues are surprisingly big.

But I threw it away and got her some water
Then stroked her hair and said sorry
I cleaned up her face, now my secrets were safe
Knowing there's no need to worry.

I know that I won't get away with all this
But if those secrets had been overflowing...
So whatever punishments Mum dishes out
Won't be half as bad as her knowing.

Outro

Come pretty much full circle now
From the tower blocks near school
We've been up past Brick Lane
Through the back streets of Globe Town
Past the gasworks to Mile End
Down to Limehouse
And now we're back where we started
It's been quite a journey, but it's time that we parted.

Thank you for sharing our burden
It's good to have handed it on
They say nothing weighs more than a secret
And secrets are measured in tonnes.

Most people think secrets are something to hide
Like rubbish that rots in your soul
But we know it's better to wash yourself clean
Cos that's how you stay in control.

Ain't sayin it's easy to pluck up the courage
To burst that bubble of fear
You're scared you'll be judged
Or even rejected
But if you stay true and sincere
You'll find that a secret comes out with a sigh
Not a scream or a gnashing of teeth
It draws people to you
Who see themselves through you
And you gasp as you share their relief.

This is the power of sharing a secret
It says: This is who I am
I'm real
I'm human
Flawed but true
Imperfect

Normal
Just like you.

And with the stitches removed, the wound has healed
The myth exploded, the truth revealed.

You see sharing the worst is what humans do best
It's how we build hope and unity
Learning to trust
Forgive
And accept
That's how we create a community.

The End.

---

1. East London pronunciation of 'Know what I'm saying?'
2. Bengali person – East London slang

THE UNRAVELLING

Author's Note

Our third production at Edinburgh, *The Unravelling*, won
Mulberry Theatre Company a Scotsman Fringe First Award, the
first time a school has ever received one. The play is in many
ways an existential fable about the power of the imagination;
the challenges it set its performers and production team are
certainly the greatest so far. It builds upon the previous two
years in that it places a metaphorical 'handover' between female
generations at the heart of the story (a subtext in *Mehndi Night*),
yet it also uses direct-address storytelling (the legacy of *Stolen
Secrets*) as the means by which the characters summon their
imaginative worlds from the apparent emptiness around them,
and in so doing, discover their power. By 2009, as artists we
had become bold enough to give the students the location – an
East London fabric shop – explain its metaphorical, other-
worldly potential, and challenge them to populate it with
spooky characters and strange goings-on.

The result is a play of mixed styles which, whilst predominantly
about a mother and her three daughters, also uses a set of
Narrators who could be played by a mixed cast. There is an
archetypal quality to this play; the lead characters do not have
names but are rather 'Mother', 'Eldest', 'Middlest' and
'Youngest', meaning that this is a story which transcends any
culturally specific context and could be set in any city,
anywhere in the world. (References to East London place
names may be replaced accordingly.) Note also that the
Narrators form a chorus of indeterminate number. In the
original production we used two, but this is the minimum it
could be done with.

Once again I owe a debt to my director and collaborator Camille
Cettina, to our designer Barbara Fuchs, and of course to our
incredible cast. Their spectacularly imaginative production was,
I am sure, the main reason we received our award.

The Unravelling was first performed on 10th August 2009 at The Space UK (Venue 45), Edinburgh, with the following cast and crew:

NARRATORS	Tamanna Hussain
	Shalma Hussain
SEAMSTRESS	Rufia Begum
MOTHER	Suhena Begum
ELDEST DAUGHTER	Rabia Begum
MIDDLEST DAUGHTER	Nurjahan Bibi
YOUNGEST DAUGHTER	Farihah Begum
Director	Camille Cettina
Assistant Director	Shona Davidson
Designer	Barbara Fuchs
Stage Management & Design	Ambia Khatun
	Nowshin Sharmeli Prenom
	Ragia Khanom
Catering	Rugina Begum
Film	Tasmin Akhtar
	Luthfa Ali
	Ruhanna Begum
	Sayeda Begum
	Fuzia Khanom

Characters

NARRATORS
SEAMSTRESS

MOTHER
ELDEST DAUGHTER
MIDDLEST DAUGHTER
YOUNGEST DAUGHTER

Narrators also play:
CUSTOMERS
DOCTOR
KING
SISTERS
REFLECTION
ZOMBIES
FISH
BIRDS

…and all other non-speaking parts and landscapes

Darkness. In the darkness, NARRATORS *speak.*

NARRATORS. This is a story about stories
About stories inside stories inside stories
Each one unravelling from the next
So many stories in fact
One on top of the other
That it's like…
Like…
Like what?
A tower block!
Nah man, that's a different kind of storey.
It's like one of them dolls
With one inside another inside another
Then just when you think you've got to the last one
You open it up
And there's one more!
Then one more
Then one more again
Brrr, I don't like that, it gives me the shivers.
Exactly
I mean, where does it all end?
Where does any of it end?
Like a patchwork that goes on for ever
Each one of us just a tiny piece.

Hang on, someone's gotta be sewing it all together.
Oh yeah, someone is
Don't worry about that
In fact, that's where our first
Story
Starts…

Lights go up to a murky semi-darkness, solely on the NAR-
RATORS. *They are huddled around a model box, which one
of them is holding like a doll's house, inside which is a scale
model of an East London fabric shop. They peer inside.*

There are tiny rolls of fabric hanging from the walls, tiny signs with prices on, a tiny till and several tiny figures – one of which is an old lady sitting at a sewing machine. Faintly, we can hear the sound as it whirrs.

And there she is
A lonely old Seamstress
In a stuffy old fabric shop
Down a dusty old alley
In a forgotten part of town.

What's she doing?
Sewing, innit
Hunched over her machine
All day and all night
Sewing suits
Saris
Skirts
Shirts
Whatever takes her fancy
The raw ingredients of life hang from her walls
Fabric
So much fabric you wouldn't believe it
Every pattern
Weave
Yarn
Stitch
Tightly packed
Waiting to be unrolled
Snipped
Ripped
Sliced
And breathed into life.

They look more closely at the model box and see a set of tiny figures, dressed exactly like them, huddled around a tiny model box. The sound of the sewing machine gets louder over the following.

Who are them other people then?
Them? I dunno
Visitors?

Customers maybe
They look familiar…
Dressed a bit like us…
Dressed a lot like us…
Dressed *exactly* like us!
I'm scared!
Wait, they're looking at something
Oh yeah, huddled round in a group
Looking at –
Looking at –
Looking at –
No way!
A box!
A model!
A tiny fabric shop!
A model inside a model inside a –
Stop it, man, this is freaking me out!

*The lights go up suddenly on the real theatre set, and we see
we are in a fabric shop EXACTLY like the one in the model
box. Rolls of fabric hang from the walls, there are signs with
prices on, a till and an old lady (the* SEAMSTRESS) *sitting
at a sewing machine. The sound of it whirring reaches a
crescendo then stops.*

The NARRATORS *all freeze, like mannequins modelling
clothes.*

The SEAMSTRESS *looks up from her work.*

SEAMSTRESS. The realisation comes to us all:
    We are all puppets
    In one titanic tale.

She claps her hands.

Drop!

The NARRATORS *become lifeless, dangling like puppets
hanging from strings.*

The SEAMSTRESS *wanders between them.*

This is a place where people come to imagine
Conjure

Reinvent
Summoning themselves
Like genies from the dust storm of life.

Harried housewives
With heavy bags and heavier hearts.
Suited secretaries
Seeking to dictate their own terms.
Sleepy students
Sick of seeming second hand.
Glamorous grannies
Grabbing one last twirl before the lights wink out.

*She drapes each lifeless 'puppet' in a piece of clothing as a
signifier of their role, e.g. a shawl for a grandmother, a suit
jacket for a secretary.*

Stepping off the conveyor
They creak open my door
And they stop
Drop
And suddenly remember to breathe.

The SEAMSTRESS *takes a deep breath and blows.*

The NARRATORS *collectively take one huge breath.*

Believe me
I see it.
I see it all.

*The puppets come to life as customers in the shop: a house-
wife, a grandmother, a secretary, a student – all quietly
browsing through different fabrics.*

As the SEAMSTRESS *continues, they enact the movements
she describes.*

They scan the rolls
One catches their eye
They stop
Step
Reach
Touch

Unravel – just a little
And it's then that the magic begins:
Imagining
A dress
A look
A life.

Here, everything is possible
And everything exists
This is a sacred place
Where they come to commune with the future.

Drop!

The NARRATORS *drop once more.*

You want stories?
I'll tell you stories
For what is life but a sprawling mass of threads
Whirling away to some distant vanishing point?

I call it 'The Unravelling'.

With the next four words she clicks her fingers in front of the
NARRATORS *and they ping back to life.*

Once
Upon
A
Time.

The SEAMSTRESS *becomes a silent character in the story*
as the NARRATORS *take over.*

They pull back a curtain to reveal four more lifeless puppets,
which they proceed to dress as the MOTHER *and three*
DAUGHTERS *during the following…*

They give the YOUNGEST *the model box, which she uses as*
a doll's house to play with.

NARRATORS. A mother ran this fabric shop with her three
     daughters
     In the east of the city
     Their little shop sandwiched between tower blocks

Like a solitary prawn between two loaves of bread
Overcrowded
Overlooked
Overcome
As the future piled up around them.
The mother was a strong woman
Proud
Independent;
She had taken over this shop from an old lady Seamstress
Who used to run it back in the day
Since for ever it seemed.

SEAMSTRESS. Since all this was fields, and London a distant cloud.

NARRATORS. Or so she said.
The Seamstress didn't seem to have any family
And she didn't talk much
Though she had a twinkle in her eye
So the mother offered to retain her in the shop
To provide a tailoring service in the back room
To those who wanted it.

Sometimes she'd produce something for the daughters:

The SEAMSTRESS *hands the following items of clothing to the* NARRATORS *to dress the* DAUGHTERS *as they mention them.*

A punky purple top for the eldest
She was a bit emo[1]
Black make-up
Black clothes
Camden's finest
Streaky hair
Pentagram jewellery
And seriously serious music
You know the sort.

ELDEST. I am cursed to walk through crowds alone
An ancient heart, forever young
My soul is made of stone.

NARRATORS. Yeah, whatever.

ELDEST *puts on an MP3 player and disappears into her music*.

Sometimes the Seamstress would make something for the
Middle daughter
Something sparkly
Girly
Glitzy
Glam
For this one had a taste for the finer things in life
Her head full of glossy magazines
Parties
Pearls
And cocktail twirls.
She lives for Saturday shopping
When the world is her Oyster card.

MIDDLEST. Yeah, but what is life about but gettin rich, yeah?
Not that I'm tryin to be a git, yeah
But how can you look good while bein poor?
I think I'd rather drown than not have more.

NARRATORS. And more and more
Keep an eye on this one, she'll rob you blind.

MIDDLEST *flicks on the TV with a remote control*.

MIDDLEST. Ah wicked, *Sex and the City*.

She watches TV.

NARRATORS. What did the youngest get?
Ah, bless the youngest
Sweet
Quiet
Not yet in her teens
She lives on chocolate
And doll's-house dreams.

The SEAMSTRESS *gives the* NARRATORS *some tiny clothes for the* YOUNGEST *to dress her dollies in*.

Here you go.

YOUNGEST. Thanks. This one's me. She's learning to fly.

YOUNGEST *makes the dolly fly.*

Neeeeeeeoooooooooooooowwwwwwwwwwwwwwwww!

NARRATORS. Anyway
　　Yeah, anyway
　　After their father had left
　　Some time ago
　　The mother had struggled to raise her daughters alone
　　And keep the business afloat
　　Especially as she was quite old-fashioned when it came to
　　fabric
　　And refused to stock any cheap synthetic material.

The MOTHER *holds up a piece of material with a beautifully
intricate design. The* NARRATORS *play the* CUSTOMERS.

MOTHER. Look at this workmanship;
　　Handmade, by the finest weavers
　　The thread so fine it is like melted gold.

CUSTOMER 1. Yeah, but it's ten ninety-nine a yard.

MOTHER. What price can you put on quality?

CUSTOMER 1. I ain't payin that.

NARRATORS. But the mother had a trick up her sleeve to
　　ensure her customers' continued loyalty;
　　With each customer that bought a few yards
　　She started to spin them a yarn.

MOTHER. Ah, this one is so beautiful – a lovely choice.

CUSTOMER 2. Thank you. It's for my daughter's wedding.

MOTHER. You know, this particular cloth reminds me of the
　　tale about the Bride who saw her future in the patterns of her
　　dress…

NARRATORS. And as she'd unravel
　　And measure
　　And snip
　　And tear
　　She'd spin out the tale
　　Detail by tantalising detail.

MOTHER....of course, her husband soon got wind of it and called her in to see him.

CUSTOMER 2. What did he say?

MOTHER. He was furious. He accused her of being a witch!

NARRATORS. And as she folded –

MOTHER. Flung her into jail...!

NARRATORS. And wrapped –

MOTHER. Wept for a thousand nights...

NARRATORS. And rang up the price –

MOTHER. Then suddenly she remembered the prophecy she had foreseen in the cloth...

NARRATORS. The customer would slowly –

MOTHER. But surely –

NARRATORS. Become bewitched by the mother's spell.

MOTHER. Four ninety-nine, please.

CUSTOMER 2. But I want to know how it ends!

MOTHER. The next chapter is included with your next purchase.

NARRATORS. And she'd send them away!
  Frustrated!
  But even better
  When they came back
  To buy more cloth
  And hear how the story ended up.

CUSTOMER 2. Last time, you were telling me about the Bride, the one who saw the future – I have to know: what happened next?

NARRATORS. The mother would smile softly and say:

MOTHER. I'm terribly sorry
  I've forgotten how that one goes.

NARRATORS. And then start all over again!

MOTHER. But this particular fabric reminds me of the one about the Most Important Letter in the World, do you know it?

CUSTOMER 2. I don't think so.

MOTHER. One day, a letter bearing no stamp arrived at the door of a starving old man...

NARRATORS. And she'd be off!
    Every time another story
    Every time unfinished
    Like a hook in the heart of everyone she served.

    The daughters mind you, were Lazy
    With a capital Lay.
    With the Eldest plugged into her iPod
    The Middlest her celebrity shows
    And the Youngest her flying dollies
    They worked in the shop under duress.

ELDEST. I wanna be in Camden.

MIDDLEST. I wanna be in New York.

YOUNGEST. Neeeeeeooooowwwwww!

NARRATORS. Cooped up in the little shop
    It wasn't long before they'd start to fight.

MIDDLEST (*to* ELDEST). Have you nicked my lipstick?

ELDEST. Why would I do that?

MIDDLEST. Have you?

ELDEST. Is it black?

MIDDLEST. What?

ELDEST. Or is it stupid girly pink?

MIDDLEST. It's pink, innit, I ain't some Goth freak.

ELDEST (*mutters*). Plastic.

MIDDLEST. You what?

ELDEST. I called you plastic, you little minger.

The MIDDLEST *is about to respond but notices the* YOUNGEST *is using her lipstick to paint her dolly's face pink.*

MIDDLEST. Oi, what are you doing?!

YOUNGEST. She flew too close to the sun, she got burnt.

MIDDLEST. Give that here, you little squirt!

The MIDDLEST *snatches her lipstick.*

It's ruined!

The MIDDLEST *whacks the* YOUNGEST.

YOUNGEST. Ow!

MOTHER. Stop it!

MIDDLEST. Don't EVER nick my stuff!

MOTHER. Stop it, all of you!

YOUNGEST. She started it.

MIDDLEST. She did.

ELDEST. She did.

MOTHER. There are customers waiting. Go and serve them.

The NARRATORS *play the* CUSTOMERS.

Each DAUGHTER *approaches a* CUSTOMER, *sulkily.*

ELDEST. Alright.

MIDDLEST. Alright.

YOUNGEST. Alright.

MIDDLEST. That'd look crap on you.

ELDEST. Have you thought about black?

YOUNGEST. You look like my dolly.

MOTHER. Not like that! Draw them in. Tell them a story.

ELDEST. There was a man, he hated life so he killed himself, six ninety-nine, please, the end.

MOTHER. No! I have worked myself to the bone keeping this shop afloat, and for what? So you can drive my customers away with your sour-faced ingratitude? I don't think so.

MIDDLEST. Yeah, but Mum, man, it's a bit embarrassing, d'you know what I mean?

MOTHER. I do not.

MIDDLEST. Tellin stories is for, like, babies.

ELDEST. Yeah.

YOUNGEST. I like stories.

MIDDLEST / ELDEST. Exactly!

YOUNGEST. Shut up!

ELDEST. It was okay when we were little and whatever –

MIDDLEST. But we're grown-up now, we live in reality, yeah?

ELDEST. Yeah!

MIDDLEST. Maybe you need to as well. You've been stuck in this place for so long, it's sent you mad.

YOUNGEST. Leave Mum alone!

MIDDLEST. Shut up, squirt.

ELDEST. You know what your problem is, Mum? You live your life through this fantasy world.

MIDDLEST. Yeah, life ain't about princesses and dragons and swords.

YOUNGEST. Yes it is.

MIDDLEST / ELDEST (*to* YOUNGEST). Shut up.

MIDDLEST (*to* MOTHER). It's real, d'ya get me? It's about iTunes and McDonald's and phones that can e-mail.

MOTHER. I pity you. You young people now exist just as loose threads, blowing in the breeze. What is going to bind you together?

MIDDLEST. Durr. *X Factor*, of course.

The CUSTOMERS *become the* NARRATORS *again*.

NARRATORS. But there was something the mother wasn't
    telling her daughters.
    Ever since their father had left, she had had a pain
    At first, she thought it was just a broken heart
    And would heal over time.
    But it didn't
    It got worse.

    She'd been having treatment
    Secretly
    Down Mile End Hospital
    First thing in the morning
    And last thing at night.
    Doctors would press and poke and enquire
    Nurses would smile and stroke and admire
    While massive machines would inject her with fire.

    MOTHER *screams silently*.

    It hurt
    Man, did it hurt
    But all the while she never breathed a word
    Staying silent
    Strong
    For the sake of her girls.

    Inside, she imagined the story:
    A molecular battlefield
    Two armies massed in opposition
    On one side the soldiers of medicine
    Neat
    Disciplined
    Obeying commands
    Armed with scalpels
    And spiky needles.
    On the other, the barbarians of disease
    Dirty
    Mindless
    Violent thugs
    With clubs
    And bats

They'd gnaw like rats
Laying waste to her very insides.

YOUNGEST. You okay, Mum?

MOTHER. Yes. Yes, I am fine.

The SEAMSTRESS *gives one of the* NARRATORS *a white coat, she becomes a* DOCTOR.

NARRATORS. Then one day
The doctor called her in
Told her
Quietly
Tenderly
It was over
The disease had won
And its prize
The spoils of its victorious war
Was to be her life.

DOCTOR. I am so terribly sorry.

NARRATORS. And all of a sudden
The lady whose stories never ended
Had her own ending imposed from above.

MOTHER. How long
How long do I have?

DOCTOR. Until sunrise tomorrow…
Less than one day.
Is there anyone I can call?

MOTHER *shakes her head.*

Go home.
Tell your children.

NARRATORS. So she did.
Shooed away the last customers
Closed the shop early
Pulled down the shutters
And gathered her daughters to her
To tell them the news.

The MOTHER *gathers her* DAUGHTERS *round in a huddle
and mimes talking to them.*

The DAUGHTERS *mime their reactions.*

It hurt
Man, did it hurt
It hurt them even more than when Dad left
Or when JLS got voted off *X Factor*
Or when the Eldest accidentally killed the family hamster by
putting him inside the printer.
It hurt a lot.

MOTHER. Stop this, please!
I am weak.
There will be plenty of time for grief
But I am not gone yet
And there is something I need each of you to do for me.

ELDEST. Anything.

MIDDLEST. Name it.

YOUNGEST. Just say.

MOTHER. I have until sunrise before the disease takes me.
I have to know that this place
Everything I have worked for
And all that we have
Will be secure.

ELDEST. It will.

MIDDLEST. Of course it will.

YOUNGEST. We'll take care of it.

MOTHER. No.
It needs a guardian
Someone who understands that all this
Is more than material
More than cloth
It is the fabric of reality itself.

The DAUGHTERS *exchange glances like the* MOTHER *has
gone a bit mad.*

Each of you will tell me a story
The most important story you will ever tell
The story that is yours, and yours alone.
The story that will decide which of you is ready.
Ready to inherit the future.

ELDEST. Not to be disrespectful or anything, Mum
But what sort of time is this for stories?

YOUNGEST. I'll do it. I don't know about the others.

MIDDLEST. I don't know any stories.

ELDEST. Me neither.

MOTHER. Look around you. Everything you need is right here.

YOUNGEST. Come on, you two. Do it for Mum.

NARRATORS. The daughters paced
And pondered
Turning over their mother's strange request
Like a smooth stone in the palm of the hand
As they sifted through the shop's many fabrics
And racked their brains for ideas.

The ELDEST *picks up some black cloth, like you might wear at a funeral.*

The MOTHER *illustrates the next speech by walking across the fabric with her fingers.*

MOTHER. The pattern is the journey, its ending foretold in its beginning.
The stitches are the steps along the way, each pricked with a spot of the maker's blood, marking her sacrifice as she goes.
The pigments are the landscapes, twisting between darkness and light as her journey unfolds.
The sequins are the omens, glittering mirrors, promising the treasure she seeks.
Beads are the boulders, a shadow of darkness behind every one.
While pockets of lace are treachery, where the ground opens up, nothing is as it seems, and she must cling on for dear life.
And finally the twist in the tale, where she must enter the

darkest folds, unravel, and be born again
For ever changed from the person she once was.
The finest stories, like the finest fabrics, are nothing less than
lessons in living.

She passes the fabric to the ELDEST, *who examines it*
despondently.

ELDEST. Why can't life be easy?

MOTHER. My eldest, you ask a profound question…

YOUNGEST. Because if we didn't struggle we wouldn't grow
up.

MOTHER. Where do you get such wisdom, little one?

MIDDLEST (*mutters*). Squirt.

ELDEST. I want mine to have a happy ending.

MOTHER. We get the endings we weave.

ELDEST. Oh, I can't do this!

MOTHER. Please. I need to see you try.

MIDDLEST. You have to try. For Mum.

YOUNGEST. It's not that hard. I tell stories to my dollies all
the time.

ELDEST. Yeah? Why don't you go first then?

MOTHER. No. You must begin. This is the burden of the eldest.

MIDDLEST. Come on, you can do this.

YOUNGEST. You've just gotta believe in what you're saying.

MOTHER (*of the* ELDEST's *fabric*). You have chosen black.
This means a journey into darkness.

ELDEST. Right.
    Alright.
    Believe…

MIDDLEST. Once

YOUNGEST. Upon

MIDDLEST. A

ELDEST. Time
 There was a girl
 Who felt... unhappy.

MIDDLEST. Why?

ELDEST. I don't know!

MOTHER. Close your eyes.
 Forget who you are.
 And fall through the hole in the yarn.

 ELDEST *closes her eyes*.

ELDEST. There was a girl
 Who felt unhappy
 Because
 Because...
 Her mum was ill
 Really really ill.
 But she'd heard there was a cure
 A potion of eternal life
 Which would make anyone who drank it immortal.
 So
 So...
 She went...

YOUNGEST. To see someone!

 The MIDDLEST *brings the* SEAMSTRESS *over.*

MIDDLEST. A vile old witch.

MOTHER (*to* SEAMSTRESS). Sorry.

ELDEST. A wise, kindly...

YOUNGEST. Ancient

MIDDLEST. Wrinkly

YOUNGEST. Old

MIDDLEST. Crone!

ELDEST. *Lady…*
Who lived deep in the heart of the forest
Epping Forest
In an old old cottage.

The tale begins to take shape now, with the NARRATORS
*becoming the forest, and various other parts and effects as
required.*

The old lady had lived there for as long as anyone could
remember
Since for ever it seemed
Never eating
Never drinking
And never growing older.
The rumours were that she was enchanted
In league with the Devil
And couldn't be killed
Or hurt.

MOTHER. Good. Go on.

ELDEST. If anyone was going to know about the potion for
eternal life
It was her.
So the girl knocked on the door
Creaked it open
And let herself in.

SEAMSTRESS. The potion you seek does exist –

ELDEST. She said, without even being asked.

SEAMSTRESS. But no one has been able to find it
Because it is made by the King of the Underground himself
And shut fast within a workman's locker
In the darkest of his dark tunnels
Deep within the earth.

ELDEST. You have to tell me how to get there!

SEAMSTRESS. Why, the door to the Underground is right here.

The SEAMSTRESS *reveals a door.*

When you get there, tell the King the Seamstress sent you.
We used to be quite good friends.

YOUNGEST. That's fishy.

ELDEST. Shut up.
So she goes through the door and down into the Underground to meet the King. When she gets there –

YOUNGEST. Hang on, it's gotta be harder than that!

MIDDLEST. Yeah!

ELDEST. What you on about?

YOUNGEST. She's got to struggle, remember?

MIDDLEST. Yeah, maybe she has to walk through slime –

YOUNGEST. Or sewage –

MIDDLEST. Or giant rats –

YOUNGEST. Or dead tramps –

MOTHER. Oh, please.

ELDEST. Look, whose story is this – mine or yours?

MIDDLEST / YOUNGEST. Yours.

ELDEST. Right, so shut up. (*To* MOTHER.) They're always
trying to take over.

MOTHER. Go on, child. (*To the others*.) It's her story, let her
tell it.

ELDEST. Right, so going down into the Tube, it's all rank and
everything
Rats and whatever
She goes through the barrier
Down the escalator
And quietly sneaks off the end of the platform
And down into the pitch-black tunnel.
It isn't long before she finds the King of the whole place
Sat on his throne, a mouldy Tube-train seat writhing with
maggots
Man, is he scary
Like a skull in a London Transport hat

The NARRATORS *animate the figure from objects in the shop.*

A cloak of – of *Metro* newspapers
And those sparks from the live rail flashing in his empty eye
sockets!
The girl feels all small and scared
And he peers down at her
And it's like being looked at by a – a ticket inspector!

MIDDLEST / YOUNGEST. Uh!

ELDEST. And when he speaks it's in this booming voice
Like through a megaphone
And he goes:

KING. WHAT IS THIS MORTAL DOING IN MY
KINGDOM? THIS IS THE KINGDOM OF THE DEAD!

YOUNGEST. Wicked!

MOTHER. Hush, child.

KING. AND WHERE IS YOUR TICKET!?

ELDEST. Luckily she'd bought one that day so she hands it over
Then she starts to explain about her mum
And the potion she needs
And how the Seamstress sent her.
But the King – the Devil (cos that's what he is really, innit)
Laughs this big evil laugh like this:

The KING *laughs a big evil laugh.*

Then he goes:

KING. I WILL GIVE YOU THIS POTION
BUT IN RETURN I REQUIRE ONE THING.

ELDEST. What?

KING. YOUR SOUL WHEN YOU DIE.

MIDDLEST. Oh no!

YOUNGEST. Don't do it!

ELDEST. But she has to do it, doesn't she!
Cos otherwise her mum will die!

So she goes, 'Alright then'
And he hands over the potion.

The KING *hands* ELDEST *a can of Red Bull which is sitting somewhere in the shop.*

MIDDLEST. Can there be a thunderclap?

ELDEST. If you like.

There is a loud thunderclap. ELDEST *takes the potion from the* KING.

Thanks then.
And she's off.

MOTHER. But –

YOUNGEST. Yeah, there's always a but.

ELDEST. Yeah, I know!
BUT
On the journey back, she gets lost
Cos she gets off at the wrong stop – Oxford Circus or somewhere like that where it's really confusing
And she can't find the door back to the World!
Taking a total shot in the dark, she goes for Exit four hundred and ninety-nine
But it's the wrong one!
And she ends up in this sewer, doesn't she
Sludgy
Gloopy
Stinky
A yellow mist hangs there like –
Like –
The smell of death.

MIDDLEST. You mean like your bedroom?

ELDEST. Shut up.

MOTHER. Yes, shush.

ELDEST. The girl's come too far to go back
But the end is nowhere to be seen
So she sits down in the stinking sewage and cries

Cos she doesn't know what else to do.
And all the time she can't stop thinking:
I sold my soul to the Devil
I sold my soul to the Devil
And when she dies she's gonna have to come back here
To this stinking godforsaken sewer
FOR EVER!
But –

MIDDLEST. But –

YOUNGEST. But –

ELDEST. She doesn't have to die, does she?
Cos she's got the potion in her pocket
The one for eternal life
The one for her mum.

YOUNGEST. Don't do it!

MIDDLEST. Yeah, but hang on, right. It's better than going to
Hell, innit. And I reckon her mum would understand. (*To*
MOTHER.) Right?

MOTHER. Quiet, I want to hear what she does.

The ELDEST *opens the can of Red Bull.*

ELDEST. So she opens it up
And knocks it back in one gulp
Like a wino in a Commercial Road pub
Just desperate for something to comfort her in the middle of
all this evil.
Then
As if by magic
(Well, it has to be by magic, doesn't it)
A door opens in the sewer wall
(Cos if you think about it, that wouldn't happen normally)
And pulling her frozen feet out of the gloop
She lunges straight for it
Dives through head first
And lands with a thump
On the floor of the old lady's kitchen
In the dark heart of Epping Forest.

SEAMSTRESS. It worked!
　　The curse has lifted!
　　I am released at last!
　　Welcome to immortality, young one.

ELDEST. And cackling like the old witch she really was –

YOUNGEST. I knew it!

ELDEST. The old lady collapses and dies
　　Released at last from her eternal life.

MIDDLEST. Yeah, but what's so wrong with living for ever?
　　I wouldn't mind it
　　Better than dying, innit.

YOUNGEST. But what about the mother?

ELDEST. Yeah, alright, I'm getting to that.
　　So it was with a heavy heart that she headed back home
　　And without telling anyone where she'd been or what she'd done
　　She watched as her family nursed their mother through her final hours
　　And she slowly slipped away.

The NARRATORS *mime this scene, and become the* SISTERS.

YOUNGEST. No!

MIDDLEST. It's alright. It's just a story.

YOUNGEST. It's sad.

ELDEST. But life kept going as it always does
　　The years breathed in and breathed out
　　Each one popping like a bubblegum ball
　　And everyone began to notice
　　The girl wasn't ageing
　　And her sisters became suspicious.

SISTERS. What's her secret?
　　Surgery I expect.
　　Botox.
　　She'll fall apart soon enough, when it wears off.

    Everything will head south.
    You wait.

ELDEST. But it didn't.
    And one by one her sisters died
    And then her friends
    And then everyone she had been to school with
    Everyone in her tower block
    And everyone she had ever met
    Until one day the girl found she was all alone in the world
    And didn't know anyone.

MIDDLEST. Actually, that is a bit crap, isn't it?

YOUNGEST. Shh.

MIDDLEST. You ssh.

MOTHER. Ssh!

ELDEST. She watches as new generations are born, grow up,
    and die
    New skyscrapers rise and fall on the London skyline
    And the Thames continues to rise.
    Her perspective on life becomes longer;
    Stretched like elastic over the years till she swears her heart
    is gonna snap.
    She grows wise
    From seeing the same mistakes again and again;
    The same violence and turf wars
    The same poverty and misery and broken lives –
    All of it unnecessary
    All of it preventable.

    The first time she tries to kill herself she does it off the top of
    a tower block
    The highest she can find
    And as she hurtles towards the cold pavement, she thinks:
    'Please let this be the end of it'
    But though she passes out when she hits the ground
    THWACK!

MIDDLEST. Ooh, nasty.

ELDEST. She wakes up the next morning in her own bed
    Alive and unhurt.

YOUNGEST. How does she do that?

MIDDLEST. Cos she lives for ever, stupid, innit
    She can't die.

YOUNGEST. Oh yeah.

ELDEST. The second time she tries it, is with a rope.
    The third time with a knife.
    The fourth in the welcoming folds of the Thames –
    But each time she wakes in her own bed.

MIDDLEST (*to* YOUNGEST). See?

ELDEST. Talk of her suicide attempts spreads throughout the
        city
    And ordinary mortals become afraid of her
    The strange woman who cannot die.
    They call her a witch
    Set fire to her flat
    And tell their children to stay away.
    Eventually
    Hounded out of every suburb and borough
    She has nowhere left to live
    But the old old cottage in Epping Forest
    Where she first found the old lady.

The door to the Underground appears.

    The door to the Underground
    Which she went through, and sealed her fate
    All those years ago
    Still shimmers in the derelict kitchen.
    Despairing of what else to do
    She steps back through it
    Thinking that maybe the Underground King has an antidote
    Or an answer
    At the very least he's someone she knows.
    When she gets there –

YOUNGEST. Through the sewage and –

ELDEST. Yeah, the rats and all that
    She gets to his mouldy throne

Throws herself at his feet and goes:
'Your Majesty! You have to tell me if there is any cure for
this curse of immortality!'
And the King raises himself up to his full height and
bellows:

KING. THERE IS ONLY ONE CURE.
BUT BEFORE I TELL YOU
YOU MUST DO SOMETHING FOR ME.

ELDEST. And the girl was so desperate she said: 'Anything!
Anything!'

YOUNGEST. Never say that to a ticket inspector.

MIDDLEST. Too right.

ELDEST. And to her horror he boomed back:

KING. YOU MUST MARRY ME!

MIDDLEST. No!

YOUNGEST. Told you.

KING. YOU ESCAPED MY CLUTCHES ONCE
I WON'T ALLOW IT AGAIN.

YOUNGEST. What did she do?

ELDEST. Married him of course.
What choice did she have?

YOUNGEST. What was it like?

ELDEST. Horrible!
It was like a funeral;
Everyone wore black
Cos everyone down there is dead, aren't they
So all the guests totally stank
And bits of them kept falling off.

MIDDLEST / YOUNGEST. Eurgh.

ELDEST. The girl had to wear a bridal veil made of penalty-
fare slips
And carry a bouquet of dead rats.

MIDDLEST / YOUNGEST. Eurgh.

ELDEST. And her wedding dress was woven from that hairy
    fluff that gathers in Underground stairwells.

MIDDLEST / YOUNGEST. Eurgh!

ELDEST. At the feast, everything was dead;
    Stinking mouldy kebabs
    Rotting boxes of half-eaten fried chicken
    A cake made of chewing-gum scrapings off the floor
    And wine glasses filled with drunk people's wee.

MIDDLEST / YOUNGEST. Eurgh!

ELDEST. Or puke.

MIDDLEST / YOUNGEST. Euuuurgh!

ELDEST. But at least you got a choice.

MOTHER. I hope this isn't one you would be telling in the
    shop.

ELDEST. Yeah, but wait till you hear what was for dessert –

MOTHER. No thank you! Just tell us the ending, please.

MIDDLEST / YOUNGEST. Oh, Mum!

MOTHER. Enough! Go on.

ELDEST. Then after it was all over
    The girl goes to the King and says:
    'I've done everything you asked for
    Now tell me the cure for my immortal curse'
    And the King tells her:

KING. THERE IS ONLY ONE CURE AND IT IS THIS:
    YOU MUST PASS THE CURSE ON TO ANOTHER
    BY MAKING THEM DRINK THE POTION
    JUST AS YOU ONCE DID.

ELDEST. And on hearing that
    The girl crumpled like cut cotton
    Folded in on herself
    And sobbed;

Her mind flying back to that moment a thousand years ago
When she'd been so stupid and selfish and scared.
And she wished
Harder than she'd ever wished for anything
That she'd put her mother first
And sacrificed her soul to save her.

But as she was lying there
Helpless as a discarded rag
She heard her mother's voice
Ripple across the centuries
And like a teardrop of strength
It hardened into steel
And condensed in her heart.

MOTHER'S VOICE. My darling eldest. Do not forget that
    every ending is also a beginning.

ELDEST. She unravelled herself from her pain
    Shook it off like a dusty old shawl
    Pulled herself up to her full height
    Looked the King dead in the eye and said:
    'I won't be doing that.
    I would rather be your bride for all eternity
    Than make another suffer as I have;
    This curse stops with me.'
    Then
    She climbed up to the empty throne next to him
    And took her place at his side.

    And that is why no one lives for ever;
    The Queen of the Underground carries that curse
    So that we don't have to.

    There is a moment of shocked silence, then the DAUGH-
    TERS *break out into applause. The* MOTHER *holds her
    arms out and the* ELDEST *goes to her.*

MIDDLEST. You did it, you did it!

YOUNGEST. That was amazing!

MOTHER. How was that?

ELDEST. That was
   That was… mad
   But I did it, didn't I?

MOTHER. You did.

ELDEST. I really did it.

MOTHER. I am proud of you.

MIDDLEST. My turn, my turn!

   The MIDDLEST *grabs some fabric – an intricate design
   with pearl sequins and other bits of bling.*

YOUNGEST. I want to go next!

MIDDLEST. No, get off, right, cos mine's brilliant, yeah
   It's about this jewellery-maker, right
   Who makes the BEST and most EXPENSIVE jewellery
   EVER.

YOUNGEST. But I wanted to go next!

MOTHER. The story has started, little one
   And there's never any stopping a story that's begun.

YOUNGEST (*disappointed*). Oh.

   She sits down.

ELDEST. Don't worry, it won't be better than mine.

MOTHER. That's enough of that.

ELDEST. It's a competition, innit?
   Well, I'm winning.

MIDDLEST. No, it'll be better than yours, right, yeah
   Cos get this – she's like the biggest richest jewellery-maker
   for miles around
   Makes necklaces for all celebrities and everything?
   She specialises in pearls
   Pearl sequins
   Pearl bracelets
   Pearl necklaces
   Pearl tiaras

    And her work gets in magazines
    And on New York catwalks
    And she is SO loaded you wouldn't believe it.

ELDEST. Big deal.

YOUNGEST. Yeah, she sounds like an idiot.

MIDDLEST. Nah, but this is the story of how she lost all that
    Cos…
    Cos someone found out her secret!

ELDEST. Okay…

YOUNGEST. Could work…

MOTHER. Go on, child.

MIDDLEST. Right
    Right okay, lemme think…

ELDEST. I thought you knew it.

YOUNGEST. She's making it up!

MOTHER. But of course!

MIDDLEST. Okay, got it, yeah
    Cos when she first started, right, she was poor
    Just an ordinary girl in an ordinary council flat.
    Her mum was a jewellery-maker, yeah
    And she'd taught her three daughters how to do it
    But they couldn't afford no gold or diamonds or rubies or
    nothing
    So they had to make jewellery out of whatever they could
    find
    Like crisp packets and fag ends and leaves.
    It was alright I suppose, but it never sold for much cos,
    y'know
    Who wants a necklace made of fag ends?

ELDEST. A tramp might.

MIDDLEST. Then one day, their mother gathered them round
    and said she had to go.

YOUNGEST. Go where?

MIDDLEST. Just away
  But for a long long time
  And she might never come back.

YOUNGEST. No!

ELDEST. It's alright, it's just a story.

MIDDLEST. The eldest sister came up with this mad idea, yeah
  To go off to the Underworld or somefing
  And get this special potion –

ELDEST. What?

MIDDLEST. But it didn't work cos she drank it herself didn't
  she, selfish cow.

ELDEST. Shut up.

YOUNGEST (*to* ELDEST). That's your story!

ELDEST. Yeah, I know, she's out of order.

MOTHER. All stories are connected.

MIDDLEST. Exactly.
  Right.
  So –
  While the eldest one was away in Hell
  Drinkin puke and whatever
  The mother set the others a test
  To see who would inherit the business.

YOUNGEST. What sort of test?

MIDDLEST. Jewellery-making of course.
  But the middle sister most wanted to win
  So she stayed up aaaaall night working on her designs.
  But it wasn't no good
  Cos it's hard to make leaves and litter and whatever look
  buff, innit.
  But she tried and tried
  And got tireder and tireder
  And she was all ready to give up
  And the sun was about to rise
  When she heard a noise

A sort of clicking
Click-clack, click-clack
It seemed to be coming from the mirror…
So she tiptoed over
And peeked inside.
Oh my gosh! You'll never guess what she saw!

YOUNGEST. What! What!

MIDDLEST. Inside the mirror
On the other side
Was HERSELF.

ELDEST. Yeah, OBVIOUSLY.

MIDDLEST. Nah, but not like, a reflection
It was like her
But not her;
Different.

YOUNGEST. How?

MIDDLEST. Harder-looking
Pinched
Stony-faced
Skin drawn tight
Almost…
Skeletal.
And these eyes
Jet black
Like lookin deep into the night
And she'd hate to say it but kinda…
Kinda ugly.

ELDEST. Maybe she'd just woken up.
I feel like that in the mornings.

MIDDLEST. Nah, because get this: the reflection was deep in
concentration
Makin jewellery!
But not just any jewellery
PEARL jewellery
All made from the finest gleamingest white pearls you had
ever seen!

Massive piles of them
And the clicking noise came from them all being threaded
onto necklaces and chokers and bracelets
In huge glittering chains.

The girl gasps.

The MIDDLEST *gasps*.

And her reflection stops working
Pauses
And looks up.
And for a second she's scared
In case she's gonna reach through the mirror and pull her
inside.

But she doesn't.
Instead
The reflection grabs a handful of finished necklaces
And holds them out
For the girl to take.

So she does
As many as she can hold
Armfuls and armfuls of them
Tiny balls of Heaven
Twinkling in the darkness
Soft to the touch
Like ocean waves
And smelling like
Smelling like
Like –

ELDEST. The ocean?

MIDDLEST. Like MONEY!
    Like riches beyond her wildest dreams!

ELDEST. Oh my days.

YOUNGEST. Is that the end?

MIDDLEST. Nah, shut up, man, course it ain't.
    She won the competition, yeah
    Easily

And inherited the business and made SO much dough
And her reputation soon spread
And everyone agreed she was the finest pearl jeweller in the
whole of Tower Hamlets.

ELDEST. Yeah, catwalks and New York, you can skip that bit.

MIDDLEST. Yeah, alright!
But all of it was cos of the mirror, wasn't it
And the girl inside it with the dead eyes;
Never eating
Never sleeping
Surrounded by snow-covered mountains of pearls
The secret to the girl's success.
So she put the mirror in an upstairs room;
Locked tight behind a huge wooden door
And didn't tell a soul.

YOUNGEST. But!

MIDDLEST. But what?

YOUNGEST. There's always a but.

MOTHER. That's right.

MIDDLEST. Yeah, alright, I'm comin to that!
BUT…

She thinks for a moment, tracing the fabric with her hand.

Got it.
One night she was fast asleep in bed
When all of a sudden there was a knock at the front door
Three knocks
Big
Loud
Scary
BANG!
BANG!
BANG!
She opened it up and Oh My God
She almost died!
Cos standin there was a crowd

Stretchin off as far as she could see
Of groaning
Rotting
Moaning
Dead
ZOMBIES!

Some ZOMBIES *appears. The* YOUNGEST *screams.*

ELDEST. Ssh, it's alright, it's not real.

MOTHER. This had better be going somewhere.

MIDDLEST. Yeah, course it is.
She tries to slam the door but they smash it down.
She tries to run upstairs but they chase her.
And she's screamin
And cryin
And desperately tryin to get the bedroom window open so
she can get out and get away –
But it's stuck!
Then she feels a cold damp hand on her back
And she's bein pulled back onto the floor
And pinned down by the droolin
Stinkin
Slimy
Dead
Corpses!
(*To* ZOMBIES.) What do you want?!

ZOMBIES. WE WANT OUR TEEEEETH!

MIDDLEST. What???
And it's only then that she realises
None of them have got any teeth!
(*To* ZOMBIES.) I didn't take your teeth! You've got the
wrong girl!
But they won't let her go.

ZOMBIES. THE MIRROOOOOR!

MIDDLEST. What?

ZOMBIES. THE GIIIIIIRL IN THE MIRROOOOOR!

MIDDLEST. No, you've made a mistake!
Cos that's pearls she's been givin me
Not teeth!

ZOMBIES. EVERY NIIIIIIGHT
YOU COME TO OUR GRAAAAAAVES
AND STEAL OUR TEEEEEEEEEEEEEETH!

MIDDLEST. No, I don't!
I ain't never been to no graves!
That girl ain't nuffing to do with me!

ZOMBIES. SHE IS YOOOOOUUUUU

MIDDLEST. No!

ZOMBIES. A REFLECTION OF YOU
A REFLECTION OF YOUR GREEEEEEEEED

MIDDLEST. And on hearin that
The girl's heart sank
Cos suddenly
It all made sense.

ZOMBIES. YOU WILL FIND ALL YOUR JEWELLERY
EVERY PIEEECE
YOU WILL TAKE BACK OUR TEEEEETH
AND YOU WILL REPLACE THEM WITH PEEAAARLS
REAL PEEEEAAAARLS
OR

MIDDLEST (*terrified*). Or what?

The ZOMBIES *take out a pair of pliers each and snap them menacingly.*

ZOMBIES. WE WILL COME BACK FOR *YOUR* TEETH!

MIDDLEST. Alright, I'll find em!

YOUNGEST. What happened next?!

MIDDLEST. Next –
Well
She had to go to Margate, didn't she
To the ocean

Cos if she was gonna replace all those teeth with real pearls
She was gonna have to start divin
Cos pearls come from oysters, innit.

YOUNGEST. What's an oyster?

ELDEST. It's like a little fish
It's flat and blue
Like an Oyster card.

YOUNGEST. Oh right.

MIDDLEST. The zombies followed her the whole way
And as she started divin down for pearls
They'd stand on the shore
Eating chips
And just watch her
With those empty eye sockets.

The sea was totally calm and still
Like swimming through a mirror;
Glidin through the smooth surface
And out the other side.
Down and down
Like sinking into herself.

She dived down as far as she could
And started searching for oysters.

She swims about gathering oysters. They are indeed flat and blue, like Oyster cards.

Two hundred
Three hundred
Four hundred oysters
Five hundred
Six hundred
More hundred oysters.
Then
She begins to notice
The fish have started to watch her
And to whisper among themselves.

Some FISH *swim into view.*

FISH. Wiggle
  Smiggle
  Tiggle piggle.

MIDDLEST. Almost like –

FISH. Giggle
  Wiggle
  Smiggle giggle.

MIDDLEST. Laughter!
  (*To the* FISH). What is so funny?

FISH. Give us a wiggle
  Giggle giggle.

  The FISH *wrap the pearl-sequinned fabric round the* MID-
  DLEST's *legs so it becomes like a mermaid's tail with scales.*

MIDDLEST. And she looks down at herself
  And to her horror
  Her legs have turned into a fish's tail!
  And touching her neck
  She feels the soft folds
  Of gills!
  I'm a fish!

FISH. Hear how she babbles
  Landlubber rabble
  What she did was unforgivable
  Unthinkable
  Just terrible
  Thieving indefensible
  Highly inexplicable
  A selfish shellfish criminal!

MIDDLEST. I'm a mermaid!
  A smelly slimy fishy mermaid!

FISH. Look at her tremble
  She knows she's in trouble.

MIDDLEST. I'll put them back!
  I'll put them all back!
  I'm sorry!

FISH. This will not be possible
　　Your burden is not minimal
　　In fact it's rather sizeable
　　You will stay here being guardable
　　Deterring other criminals.

MIDDLEST. Nooooo!
　　I want to go home!
　　But they swam off
　　Giggling to themselves
　　Leaving the girl to guard the oysters she had once so self-
　　ishly plundered.

　　Left all alone
　　She sits at the bottom of the sea
　　As far above her
　　The moon begins to rise
　　Like a watery pea
　　In a sky she knew she'd never see again.

　　The girl began to sniff
　　Then weep
　　Then sob
　　Then howl
　　Pulling the ocean into her in great torrents of blue
　　And blasting it back out again
　　And her grief begins to churn up the sea.

　　And this is why
　　Twice a day
　　At sunrise and moonrise
　　Great tides sweep the once-calm ocean
　　And crash onto the land as waves.

　　Over time
　　The land dwellers put this strange event down to the moon
　　and the sun
　　But really
　　It is the jewellery-maker at the bottom of the sea
　　Hellraiser
　　Pearl thief
　　Now guardian of the oysters
　　Sobbing for her lost life.

The SISTERS *applaud. The* MOTHER *holds her arms out and the* MIDDLEST *goes to her. The* MOTHER *is visibly weaker than before.*

YOUNGEST. That was amazing!

ELDEST. It was pretty good.

YOUNGEST. She kicked your butt!

ELDEST. Shut up.

YOUNGEST. She did.

ELDEST. I'll kick *your* butt.

MOTHER (*to* MIDDLEST). You have made me very happy.

MIDDLEST. Thanks, Mum.

The MIDDLEST *notices that the* MOTHER *is becoming weaker.*

Are you okay?

YOUNGEST. My turn, my turn!

YOUNGEST *grabs a fabric, a vibrant, yellowy-orangey one.*

MOTHER (*to* MIDDLEST). I am fine. Let me hear the final tale.

YOUNGEST. Once upon a time
A little servant girl was asked by her Queen
To find the most beautiful thing in the land
The magic land of Tower Hamlets
As a gift to the husband she was going to marry.

The husband was a King from a faraway country in the north
Called Cam-den
A dark and frosty land, where the sun never rose
And everything was shrouded in darkness and ice.
They loved each other very much
Even though they were total opposites
And the Queen wanted to give him something that would
welcome him to her Queendom
And celebrate the joining of their two lands.

So the little servant girl is sitting in the palace garden
Wondering where she could look for the most beautiful thing
in the land
When a tiny baby pigeon lands on her shoulder and starts to
tweet:

BIRD. Up there! Up there!

YOUNGEST. The girl looks up
But all she can see is rooftops sprawled out ahead of her
Like a terracotta mountain range
And the huge point of Canary Wharf Tower on the horizon.
Maybe the beautiful thing would be seen from up there?
So she sets off out of the park and gets the DLR to Canary
Wharf.

At the bottom of the skyscraper, security won't let her use
the lift
So she has to climb the fire escape round the back
The climb is steep
Thousands of hard metal stairs
She climbs all day
And all night
Until finally
Just as the sun is rising
She clambers to the top of the skyscraper's highest point
The very tip of the flashing light
Sending bolts of pure white into the dawn sky, like –
Like –

ELDEST. Lightning!

YOUNGEST. Like London's pulse!

MIDDLEST (*to* ELDEST). That's better.

YOUNGEST. The wind pulls at her hair
And the height makes her sway
But she looks out over the entire Kingdom of Tower Hamlets
Glistening in the dawn light;
She can see all the way to its green edges
Where the city ends and the strange land of Country Side
begins.

It's very beautiful, but what part of it could she possibly take back for her Queen to wrap and give to the King?

Once more the little pigeon lands and tweets:

BIRD. Up there! Up there!

YOUNGEST. Up where, Birdie?
Cos all she can see above her is sky.
She reaches out for it but can't get anywhere near.

BIRD. Up there! Up there!

YOUNGEST. I'm trying!
With all her strength she tries to fly
Nnnnnnng!
But nothing happens.

Then
Remembering some wise words which her mother had once said
About forgetting who you are
And falling through the hole
She closes her eyes
Tries to forget that she can't fly
And tries to fall through the hole in the sky.

Bit by bit, she clears everything from her mind
Every thought
Every feeling
Every hope
Every longing
And begins to forget;
Forget that she is a cumbersome human being
Forget that she is a body made of flesh and blood
And slowly
But surely
She begins to take off.

In the sky, surrounded by sunlight and birdsong and cries of:

BIRDS. Up there, up there!

YOUNGEST. She turns herself towards the sun and flies into its light

Swallowed up by its warmth so she can no longer tell
Where her body ends and the universe begins.

And no one ever heard from her or ever saw her ever again.

ELDEST. Is that the end?

MIDDLEST. That's weird.

MOTHER. Shush, let her finish.

YOUNGEST. After a while
The Queen began to wonder where her servant girl had gone.
As her wedding day approached, she became concerned
And sent out a search party.
They tracked her through the rooftops
Up the fire escape
To the pulsing light above the city
But from there they could find no trace of her.

On their wedding night
The Queen's new King thought it odd that his wife hadn't
got him a gift
But being from Cam-den, he was a kind man
Who didn't care much about material things
So he said nothing of it.

Then
That night
The servant girl came to the Queen in a dream, just before
dawn.
She told her:
'Wake the King
And take him into the garden
To give him his present.'

Together, they watch the sun come up over the skyscrapers
Over the park
Over the rooftops
And flood the world with gold.

And out of nowhere
A whole flock of little pigeons
Is suddenly all around them
And every one of them tweeting:

BIRDS. Up there! Up there!

YOUNGEST. And they look up
  At the line in the dawn sky
  Where the darkness meets the light
  A patch of the sky where their two worlds meet
  Like fingers interlocking
  Cam-den
  And Tower Hamlets.

  The Queen leans over and whispers into the King's ear:

QUEEN. This is your gift.

YOUNGEST. And he looks around him
  Surrounded by beauty
  And he smiles
  And he loves her even more than he already did.

  A moment's silence. Then the others clap.

MIDDLEST. Ah, that's so sweet.

ELDEST. I don't get it. What happened to the servant girl?

  The MOTHER *holds out her arms to the* YOUNGEST*, who goes to her.*

MIDDLEST. She became a pigeon, innit
  Or something.

  The MOTHER *and* DAUGHTERS *mime the rest of their conversation, while the* NARRATORS *become* NARRATORS *again.*

NARRATORS. And as they talked
  And congratulated
  And interpreted
  It was almost as if they had been there a thousand years
  Putting off the dawn
  Their mother's disease
  And even putting off Death himself.
  But morning light danced through the curtains
  And dread closed its fingers around the Sister's hearts;
  For they knew it was time.

MOTHER. Enough.

YOUNGEST. No!

MIDDLEST. Please not yet.

ELDEST. Don't leave us.

MOTHER. I must.

ELDEST. Why?

MOTHER. It is written.

MIDDLEST. By who?

MOTHER. If I could tell you that, I would not be leaving.

YOUNGEST. We'll rewrite it!

ELDEST. Yeah! Change the ending!

MOTHER. This is not possible.
    My story has reached its final yard.
    There is nothing left but a cardboard tube.
    I'm sorry.
    Know that I love you all
    And will always be nearby.

NARRATORS. And as the Mother spoke these words
    A door to the Underground shimmered open on the shop
    floor
    And its creak
    Seemed to call her name.

    The SEAMSTRESS *operates the door.*

YOUNGEST. No!

ELDEST. Please!

MIDDLEST. Wait!
    You haven't told us who's won.

ELDEST (*to* MIDDLEST). What?
    How can you even be thinking about that?!

MOTHER. No, she is right. My ending would not be complete
    without that.

The answer is this:
Between you, you have told me everything I needed to hear.

She turns to the ELDEST.

My troubled Eldest, you will learn to control your dark soul.
It will lead you to take on burdens, and to suffer, but always
so that others may be spared.

She turns to the MIDDLEST.

My lost Middle Daughter, you will learn from your lust for
material things, and become a guardian of purity and truth.
Your sacrifice will harness the waves.

She turns to the YOUNGEST.

And my innocent baby, yours is a spiritual path, at one with
the world and everything in it. You see beauty in all things.
Your faith will unite even opposites.

MIDDLEST. But who gets the shop?

The MOTHER *smiles.*

MOTHER. Just as this fabric shop was my world
The world is *your* fabric shop now
Packed full of raw materials
From which to sew your lives.

The MOTHER *steps through the door to the Underworld,
and disappears.*

NARRATORS. And with that
She stepped across the threshold
And was gone.

A wind begins to blow. It gets stronger and stronger.

But as their mother vanished
At that very moment
A great wind hurled itself into the shop
Slamming through the front door
Chucking over chairs
Whipping at words
Wrenching at reality itself
And flinging the fabric free!

SEAMSTRESS. The Unravelling!

Every single roll of fabric on the set spontaneously comes undone and unravels down the walls and across the floor.

The wind howls so the NARRATORS *have to shout over it.*

NARRATORS. And as the cloth falls from the walls!
The fabric of reality goes with it!
A kaleidoscope of pieces!
Sequins!
Beads!
Pigments!
Patterns!
And lace!

The Sisters watch as the walls of the shop dissolve around them
And before they know it
The entire building has disappeared
The pieces of their patchwork lives lie scattered around them
And they are standing
Breathless
In the empty street where the shop once stood.

And as they turn and head down Commercial Road
Towards the distant promise of an East London sunrise
They suddenly see the rest of their lives
Stretching away ahead of them
Unravelling
Towards some distant vanishing point.

The YOUNGEST, MIDDLEST *and* ELDEST *become mannequins again.*

The SEAMSTRESS *steps out of the shadows.*

I don't get it
Yeah, how can the walls vanish?
Yeah, what the hell?
Man, that was the weirdest story I ever heard
Me too
So it wasn't a competition for the shop at all?

SEAMSTRESS. No
It was always more important than that;
It was a test of their readiness to leave it behind.

NARRATORS. What's she on about?
I dunno.
(*Whispers.*) I think she's a bit – (*Taps side of head.*) y'know.

SEAMSTRESS. There are places in life where one becomes stuck
Until one is ready to move on.

NARRATORS. Like us!
Yeah, that's a point
Yeah, we've been here ages
When do we get to go?

SEAMSTRESS. When you're ready.
It is not yet time for your own Unravelling.

NARRATORS. What about you?
Yeah, when do you get out of here?

SEAMSTRESS. Me?

NARRATORS. Yeah.

SEAMSTRESS. I left long ago
I'm here
But also there
I'm everywhere;
I am the Seamstress.

The NARRATORS *are about to speak again, but the* SEAM-STRESS *claps her hands.*

Drop!

The NARRATORS *dangle like lifeless puppets.*

Just one question remains:
Who sewed me?

The YOUNGEST *appears. She holds her model-box doll's house and is playing with the* SEAMSTRESS *figure, who she speaks to.*

YOUNGEST. Drop!

> *The* SEAMSTRESS *dangles like a lifeless puppet, both in the box and onstage.*

> *The* YOUNGEST *makes some final adjustments to the positions of the puppets in the doll's house before drawing a little curtain across.*

And they all lived happily ever after.
The End.

Blackout.

The End.

---

1.   Teen fashion style, similar to a Goth

THE URBAN GIRL'S GUIDE TO CAMPING

Author's Note

The first of Mulberry Theatre Company's productions to premiere in London, this play is a new direction for the company and its work. Rather than being developed through practical workshops with school-age students, *Urban Girl* was the result of a series of round-table discussions with a specially convened Advisory Committee of former Mulberry students (and some staff), mostly young women in their early twenties, either at university or starting careers. Rather than 'training the group up' as potential performers for the show, these meetings were much more of a discussion among equals about what this year's play could be. Chaired with wit and warmth by my collaborator Luke Kernaghan, these weekly meetings were a delight; by turns lively, heated, poignant and laugh-out-loud funny.

For my part, I started with a provocation. I put it to the committee that representations of young British Asian women in our media were woefully lacking; they were either oppressed, exotic, or (occasionally) extremists – or the wives or sisters of extremists. This simply didn't chime with anything I had experienced at Mulberry in the four years I had been there. We agreed to do something about it. This honest discussion about how best to use this opportunity to speak to a mainstream audience, in a way brought us full circle, back to the way we had developed *Mehndi Night* – just us and a committee of East London's young women, with nothing more than a blank canvas, and a desire to imprint it with something extraordinary.

The result, in both this play and the others, will I hope go some way towards doing justice to the charm, resilience and modernity of the young women of Mulberry School. They have been an inspiration and a delight for the past four years, and not one of these plays would have been possible without them. Long may they, and their theatre company, continue.

The Urban Girl's Guide to Camping was first performed on 14 July 2010 at Southwark Playhouse, London, with the following cast:

PARVIN	Rumi Begum
THAMANNA	Rumina Kamal
RAJNA	Farzana Parvin
SABINA	Sultana S. Jahan

The part of GIRL *was still being cast at the time of going to press.*

Director	Luke Kernaghan
Designer	Barbara Fuchs

I am also grateful to the Advisory Committee of Mulberry alumni and staff who gave so generously of their time in developing ideas for the play with me: Afsana Begum, Nasima Begum, Noorzahan Begum, Rasma Begum, Rumi Begum, Shanaz Begum, Sarah Dickson, Shara Ismail, Dipa Khatun, Asma Rahman, Shunita Rahman, Nilima Sahu, Farzana Shipa, Najiba Sultana, Rouni Sultana and Jill Tuffee.

Characters

SABINA, *twenty, practical, confident, slightly boyish. Beginning a career as a writer and magazine columnist. The only character who speaks to the audience*

THAMANNA, *twenty, glamorous, feminine, cocky attitude. A beautician, amateur singer, and part-time PCSO (Police Community Support Officer)*

RAJNA, *twenty-one, forthright, articulate, an imposing presence. A feminist academic and activist about to start an MPhil and university career*

PARVIN, *nineteen, small, shy, pretty but not confident. Works as a receptionist for a Canary Wharf firm, though about to give it up to get married*

GIRL, *non-speaking, seven or eight. It is important that she is played by a real child and is not imaginary.*

Notes

All the characters are second- or third-generation British Bengali Muslims from Tower Hamlets, East London.

The locations vary between flats in Tower Hamlets, and Ashdown Forest in Sussex.

The time is 2010, early summer.

Translations throughout the text are marked 'Sylheti', the dialect of Bengali from the Sylhet region of Bangladesh – which is the most widely spoken in East London.

All the characters are onstage. THAMANNA, RAJNA *and*
PARVIN *are busy packing clothes and other gear for camping*
(*not all of it appropriate*) *into large backpacks.*

SABINA *sits nearby typing onto a laptop. She stops, looks up,
and speaks to the audience. At some point during the following
she closes the laptop and joins the others in getting ready.*

SABINA. This is a story about my best friends in the whole
      wide world
   About life
   About growing up
   And about how something awful happened between us
   But also something brilliant
   And weird
   But in a kind of awful way
   Man
   I'm not telling this very well
   Start again

   What you have to understand is that I'm not really here
   And neither are they
   I'm in my room at home
   Writing all this down
   That's what I do
   I write
   It started as a blog
   A girl blog at uni
   Agony aunt, that sort of thing
   Then the student paper
   Then the odd magazine
   And here I am
   Scraping a living
   Who'd have thought?
   Not me
   I hated English in school
   And it's well scary

Cos who the hell am I?
Just some girl
Life's weird
Anyway
That's why I've started this book
Sort of a book
A guidebook
And a story
My first

What a crap beginning
I'll redo it later

Anyway here it is
The Urban Girl's Guide to Camping
It's about…
It's about everything
Everything that happened

It goes like this:

Rule One: Nature is powerful. And writing is a force of nature. You're conjuring something out of nothing – like a storm. Writing about your friends is like venturing into the wilderness, so make sure you're all protected. Change the names. Change their jobs. Change their personalities. Man, change everything. They'll still be there, in spirit. But life is too short, and the journey too long, to risk doing it any other way.

THAMANNA *is packing some hair straighteners*.

RAJNA. Hair straighteners?

THAMANNA. Yeah, why not? You can all borrow em.

RAJNA. And where are you gonna plug those in?

THAMANNA *holds up a bulky solar-powered charger.*

THAMANNA. Solar-powered charger.

PARVIN. You think of everything.

RAJNA. Where did you get that?

THAMANNA. My brother.

PARVIN. Your brother thinks of everything.

SABINA (*to audience*). So I'm not saying these people are real
  They're not
  I've just made them up
  This one here –

She goes over to THAMANNA.

  Let's call her Thamanna
  Yeah
  I like that name
  I've never met Thamanna
  But I may as well have
  Cos she's like a lot of people I know
  A contradiction
  A beautician by day
  On her days off she works for the police as one of those
  Pretend Officers.

THAMANNA. They ain't pretend!

SABINA. What are they then?

THAMANNA. They're real.

SABINA. PCSOs?

THAMANNA. Yeah.

SABINA. My brother says it stands for Pretend Coppers Sod Off.

THAMANNA. Yeah, well, Abdul hardly spends his time on the
  right side of the law, does he?

Small pause. SABINA *is hurt.*

  Sorry.

PARVIN. Do they not mind that you're a beautician as well?

THAMANNA. Why would they? I do everyone's nails back at
  the station.

PARVIN. Even the boys?

THAMANNA. *Especially* the boys. Any time you get arrested in Tower Hamlets, check his nails. They'll be perfect. That's me, that is.

SABINA. I'll tell my brother.

PARVIN. Wouldn't they rather you were, I dunno, a professional boxer or something?

THAMANNA. It's not all about beating people up, you know.

PARVIN. Isn't it?

THAMANNA. Course not. It's about the community.

RAJNA. Leave Tham alone. I think it's great. Why can't a girl be a beautician and a policewoman?

PARVIN. PCSO.

SABINA. Pretend Officer.

THAMANNA. Shut up.

PARVIN. And a singer!

THAMANNA. That's right – next *X Factor*, you wait, you just wait. (*She sings a line from a popular song.*)[1]

RAJNA. Thamanna's the ultimate feminist: glamorous, and uniformed.

THAMANNA. You make me sound like a stripper.

RAJNA. Now that would *not* be cool.

PARVIN. But isn't the police, like, full of racist idiots?

RAJNA. All the more reason to join it. How else is it gonna change?

THAMANNA. Exactly.

RAJNA. Put it there, sis.

THAMANNA *and* RAJNA *high five*.

THAMANNA. Plus, some of em are quite fit.

RAJNA. Thamanna!

THAMANNA. What?

RAJNA. That's just undermined everything!

THAMANNA. Has it? Why?

PARVIN. I still think it's weird.

RAJNA. Look, I don't like the police either, but if I was gonna be arrested I'd rather it was by Thamanna than some meat-head. Fit or not.

SABINA. What would you be arrested for, Raj?

RAJNA. Er, being Muslim? Exercising my freedom of speech? Non-violent protest?

SABINA. I thought that was allowed.

RAJNA. Not any more it isn't. Look around you.

THAMANNA. Them non-violent protestors are the worst. *So* aggressive.

RAJNA. We have every right to aggressive non-violent protest!

SABINA (*to audience*). This one here, let's call her Rajna
She's not real either
But as a type, she's out there, believe me.
Rajna's a bit of a radical, in that feminist way –

RAJNA. Yeah, I can hear you, you know.

SABINA. Well, you are, innit.

RAJNA. I'm an academic activist; a polemical poetess.

SABINA. Oh right.

RAJNA. Words are my weapons, my wit is my whetstone on which I sharpen my... my...

SABINA. Your what?

RAJNA. Something else beginning with 'sh'. I haven't finished writing that one yet.

PARVIN. 'Sheep'?

RAJNA. 'On which I sharpen my sheep'? What am I, Bo Peep?

THAMANNA. Shoes?

RAJNA. That makes *no* sense.

THAMANNA. Yeah, like, really sharp shoes. Like stilettos.

RAJNA. They're about men's fantasies, there's no place for stilettos in the revolution.

   THAMANNA *is just packing a pair of stilettos.*

THAMANNA. Not even for stabbing men through the eye?

RAJNA. We're non-violent, remember.

THAMANNA. Stabbing men through the eye non-violently then.

RAJNA. And how would that work?

THAMANNA. Really slowly... and sensuously... while singing a song. (*She sings a line of another song.*[2])

RAJNA. I despair, I really do.

SABINA. Tell em what your MPhil's gonna be in, Raj.

RAJNA. The masculisation of feminist iconography.

THAMANNA. Catchy.

RAJNA. It's a 20,000-word thesis, not a song lyric.

SABINA (*to audience*). And finally, there's Parvin. Little Parv. The baby of the group. There's a big part of me in her... but we'll get onto that later. Right now, we're just excited cos – against all the odds – Parv is the first of us to get engaged.

THAMANNA. I am SO EXCITED!!!

PARVIN. Thanks, Tham.

THAMANNA. Aren't you?

PARVIN. Yeah, I guess.

THAMANNA. It's gonna be *brilliant*! You'll, like, *officially* be my sister!

RAJNA. Sister-in-*law*.

THAMANNA. Yeah, don't nit-pick, Miss MPhil. You know how it is, she's joining the family. We can do each other's hair, go shopping, I'll do your nails and eyebrows –

PARVIN. What's wrong with my eyebrows?

THAMANNA. Nothing, they're lovely. But you gotta keep an eye on em.

SABINA. Isn't it a bit weird though, Tham?

THAMANNA. Why?

SABINA. Well, it's like, your brother and everything?

THAMANNA. No *way*. Salim is like, the nicest guy *ever*.

PARVIN. Mashallah[3].

RAJNA. That is true.

SABINA. If Raj thinks that then he must be.

RAJNA. Shut up.

THAMANNA. Mum did *such* an amazing job with him. But I always thought, right, *cos* he was so nice, he'd end up with, you know, some nasty, manipulative cow –

RAJNA. What? Why did you think that?

THAMANNA. I dunno, someone who'd take advantage of him, mess him around.

SABINA. Protective little sis.

THAMANNA. Yeah, maybe, a bit. But this way, there's no risk at all. He's marrying my best mate!

SABINA. I thought I was your best mate.

RAJNA. I thought I was.

THAMANNA. Oh my gosh, seckle[4], ladies! *One* of my best mates, alright? (*To* PARVIN.) And he is *so* into you.

PARVIN. Really?

THAMANNA. It might be arranged but, oh my gosh. I am sick of hearing your name, girl!

SABINA. Ah, that's so sweet.

RAJNA. I prefer 'assisted' to 'arranged' in this day and age.

THAMANNA. Whatever.

PARVIN. I really like him too.

SABINA. You must do, it was well quick.

PARVIN. And your parents, my God, they are so nice.

THAMANNA. We're gonna be sisteeeers!

RAJNA (*to* PARVIN). Is it true you're gonna give up your job?

PARVIN. Yeah. Yeah, it is.

THAMANNA. Quite right too, it's a crap job.

RAJNA. Thamanna!

THAMANNA. It is though!

PARVIN. It's alright.

THAMANNA. It's pressing a big red button to open a door all day. Beep – hello. Beep – goodbye.

PARVIN. There's a bit more to it than that.

THAMANNA. Look, the point is, work's boring. Let Salim earn the dollars, then we can go shopping.

RAJNA. You gonna have kids?

THAMANNA. Yeah, course.

RAJNA. It's not up to you, Tham!

PARVIN. I dunno. Can we talk about something else?

SABINA. Like what?

THAMANNA. Ah, Parv's getting all shy. It doesn't hurt, you know.

SABINA. What?

RAJNA. Thamanna!

THAMANNA. Or not as much as they say anyway.

SABINA. How would you know?

THAMANNA. I've been told.

RAJNA. Oh my gosh, Thamanna – have you – ?

THAMANNA. No, I said I've been *told*!

PARVIN (*with force*). And I said please can we talk about something else!

Pause.

THAMANNA. Alright, keep your wig on.

PARVIN. It's just – it's private.

RAJNA. That's fair enough.

SABINA. What do you wanna talk about?

PARVIN. I dunno. Camping. We're supposed to be going camping.

PARVIN *goes to her backpack and rather sulkily continues packing.*

The others exchange a glance.

A silence.

SABINA (*to audience*). Rule Two: Check the weather. Seriously. You know that saying about the calm before the storm? That silence where in that moment every sound, every movement seems magnified? Almost like the future is echoing down to you? Well, when that happens – check the weather. I mean it. Cos you just know there's gonna be a storm.

THAMANNA. What is camping anyway?

RAJNA. You know what camping is, we went in school.

THAMANNA. Did we?

SABINA. Yeah, in Year 9, to Ashdown Forest.

RAJNA. It's where the Winnie-the-Pooh stories are set.

SABINA. Durr, that's why we're going back there?

THAMANNA. Oh, that!

SABINA. Yeah, that. Where we all stayed in tents.

RAJNA. Keep up.

THAMANNA. Tents? I thought they were Wendy houses.

SABINA. They're called tents when you're a grown-up.

THAMANNA. That was camping?

SABINA / RAJNA. Yeah.

THAMANNA. That was alright, that was.

SABINA. Yeah, it wasn't proper camping though.

RAJNA. Alright, Miss Duke of Edinburgh Award.

SABINA. More like little girls running round screaming.

RAJNA. What, we're gonna be more like the SAS this time, are we?

PARVIN. What's SAS?

RAJNA. Ask Commander Begum over there.

SABINA. Look, all I know is I ain't staying up all night screaming.

RAJNA (*salutes*). Yes, sir, Sabina, sir!

THAMANNA. Hey, you're quite good at that, maybe you should join the army.

RAJNA. Yeah, right.

SABINA. At ease, soldier.

RAJNA. Get lost.

THAMANNA. Hey, do you remember, we stayed up all night telling ghost stories, and in the morning, everyone had lost their voice!

SABINA. Exactly – that hurt. I had a sore throat for, like, two weeks.

THAMANNA. Sounded like zombies – (*She does an impression.*) Bleurgh!

RAJNA. Oh – and Darren Allfield got his foot stuck in the chemical toilet!

ALL. Oh yeah!

THAMANNA. And Miss Turner had to pull him out!

PARVIN. That was funny, he fancied her so much.

SABINA. That was just a campsite anyway. Pretend camping for little girls. This time, we're going properly into the forest.

THAMANNA *holds up two different dresses.*

THAMANNA. Polka dots or stripes?

SABINA. Dresses are totally not appropriate for camping, T.

RAJNA. This is Thamanna we're talking about. Who's it for anyway, the wolves?

THAMANNA. Oh my God, there's wolves?

SABINA. No there ain't.

THAMANNA. I ain't going if there's wolves.

PARVIN. Aren't there bears in forests?

RAJNA. No, Parv. That's American forests.

THAMANNA. What about Winnie-the-Pooh?

SABINA. He wasn't real.

THAMANNA. Then why was there a book about him?

SABINA. Oh my days. Do you believe Harry Potter's real?

THAMANNA. Dunno. Might be.

RAJNA. I still swear my parents hid my Hogwarts acceptance letter back in Year 7.

SABINA. You got into Cambridge, wasn't that enough?

RAJNA. Bit less magic.

SABINA. Anyway, Winnie-the-Pooh is hardly a scary bear, is he?

THAMANNA. He'll be older now though, innit. Bigger. More dangerous.

SABINA. Oh man. Yeah, he might've got into beatboxing and drugs.

RAJNA. Just don't take any honey, he'd mug you for it.

THAMANNA. I'd stab him up. Ain't no one getting my honey.

PARVIN. You'd stab Winnie-the-Pooh? You cow.

SABINA. Look, we're getting off the point.

RAJNA. What is the point?

THAMANNA. Yeah, how the hell did you talk us into this, Sab? I'm gonna have to go without McDonald's for a whole twenty-four hours.

SABINA. Camping's deep. Especially for city girls. Life can take over. And it will – it's about to. We're almost grown up.

RAJNA. I am grown up.

THAMANNA. Yeah, and me.

PARVIN. Me too.

THAMANNA (*to* PARVIN). No you're not.

SABINA. Forget families, forget careers, forget fiancés. Camping strips all that away. This is our little window of opportunity. *Our* time. Out there, it's just you, your best friends, and the wilderness.

THAMANNA. I still don't see why we couldn't go to Chessington World of Adventures.

SABINA. Camping strips you down. It brings you closer.

THAMANNA. Don't get me wrong, I love you guys, but I ain't stripping down for no one.

SABINA. I mean it makes you ask hard questions of yourself.

THAMANNA. Like what?

SABINA. Like… can I survive without Facebook?

RAJNA *puts her iPhone into her backpack.*

RAJNA. iPhone.

SABINA. Without make-up?

THAMANNA *puts a make-up bag into her backpack.*

THAMANNA. Chanel gift set.

SABINA. In complete silence?

PARVIN *bops along to a song on her MP3 player.*

PARVIN. Aw, I love this song so much.

SABINA (*to audience*). Sometimes, I wonder whether this lot are gonna make it out alive.

PARVIN *sings a line from one of Disney's Winnie-the-Pooh songs.*

(*To* PARVIN.) No, no, stop that –

PARVIN *sings a bit more.*

Stop it, stop it!

PARVIN. Why?

SABINA. That song's copyrighted.

PARVIN. But I brought the whole soundtrack.

SABINA. Yeah, and you can't sing it, any of it. Disney won't let me put it in.

PARVIN. Oh, please.

SABINA. I'll get sued.

PARVIN. I'm the one singing it.

SABINA. Yeah, but you're not real.

PARVIN. Yeah I am.

RAJNA. Disney ruined those stories. Such a shame.

SABINA. I know, the originals are so much better.

PARVIN. What originals?

SABINA *gets out an original copy of A.A. Milne's* The House at Pooh Corner.

RAJNA. Oh, you've got it!

SABINA. Same copy I've always had.

THAMANNA. Let's have a look!

They gather round.

Oh, we're gonna have to play Poohsticks!

RAJNA. And climb a tree!

PARVIN. And catch a Heffalump!

THAMANNA. Aren't they quite scary?

PARVIN. Yeah, I don't think I wanna catch a Heffalump actually.

THAMANNA. Parv, you're like Piglet.

PARVIN. No I'm not.

THAMANNA. Yeah you are. Scared of everything.

PARVIN. Piglet was brave really.

THAMANNA. Nah, he just pretended to be.

RAJNA. What's the difference?

SABINA (*to* THAMANNA). That'd make you Tigger then.

THAMANNA. How?

SABINA. Hyperactive.

RAJNA. Yeah, and never shuts up.

THAMANNA. Shut up.

PARVIN (*to* RAJNA). Who are you then?

THAMANNA. Eeyore – grumpy cow.

SABINA. Nah, Raj has gotta be Rabbit. Clever and busy and never any time.

RAJNA. Hey, I've made time for this!

PARVIN. Which leaves Sabina. Hmmm.

RAJNA. She's gotta be Pooh.

SABINA. Why?

RAJNA. A bear of very little brain.

SABINA. Leave it out! I'm more like Christopher Robin.

RAJNA. Why?

THAMANNA. Like a boy?

SABINA. No! Because... because... it doesn't matter.

    (*To audience*.) I was gonna say: 'Because you're all my characters.' But they wouldn't have understood.

PARVIN. I'm scared.

RAJNA. Aw, Parv, we'll look after you.

THAMANNA. Piglet.

SABINA (*to audience*). Rule Three: an adventure into the great unknown is not complete without a bit of fear. Write them all down and talk about them. You'll soon see how silly they are.

PARVIN. Lions.

RAJNA. Badgers.

THAMANNA. Aliens.

RAJNA. Perverts.

PARVIN. Farmers.

RAJNA. Skunks.

THAMANNA. Owls.

SABINA. Owls?

THAMANNA. Yeah, they really creep me out, the way they can do that thing with their heads. (*She tries to do it.*) I can't do it but you know what I mean.

PARVIN. Spiders.

SABINA. My brother Abdul used to be really scared of spiders which, you know, isn't very manly. All his friends took the piss out of him for it. Do you know how he cured himself? Started eating them.

ALL. Eurgh!

SABINA. Yep. Every spider he saw, he used to make himself eat it.

THAMANNA. Your brother's mental, Sab.

SABINA. No, he's just…

RAJNA. What?

THAMANNA. Mental.

RAJNA. No. In a bad place. I pray for him. We all do.

THAMANNA. I don't.

RAJNA. Well, you're gonna start.

THAMANNA. He's always trying to hit on me.

RAJNA. Stop it, T.

THAMANNA. I'm sorry, but he is a bit sleazy.

RAJNA. Alright, enough.

SABINA. Listen, time's getting on. We need to make a move. Saddle up, ladies.

They put their backpacks on. They are very heavy.

THAMANNA. Oh my gosh!

PARVIN. Oh man.

RAJNA. That weighs a tonne!

THAMANNA. That is gonna kill me!

PARVIN. I can't even pick mine up.

SABINA. You still want five different outfits, hair straighteners and a solar-powered charger?

THAMANNA. Yeah, alright, point taken.

SABINA *hands them each a large bottle of water.*

SABINA. Take that instead.

THAMANNA. That's massive. I ain't carrying that.

SABINA. You have to.

THAMANNA. Why?

SABINA. You'll need it.

THAMANNA. Can't we just use a tap?

SABINA. Thamanna, there aren't any taps in the forest.

THAMANNA. Aren't there?

SABINA. No.

THAMANNA. What do all the animals do?

SABINA. Oh my gosh – are you serious?

THAMANNA. Look, don't start, Nature Girl. I ain't never left London, innit. 'Cept to Bangladesh but that hardly counts.

RAJNA. How would an animal turn a tap on, Thamanna?

THAMANNA. I dunno. With its teeth.

SABINA. There aren't any taps, so take that unless you wanna die of thirst.

(*To audience*.) Rule Four: Give yourself a team name. Every team needs a team name.

RAJNA. Really? Why?

SABINA. Cos we're going out there, conquering the world.

THAMANNA. Like in *The Apprentice*.

RAJNA. So what we gonna be called?

THAMANNA. Synergy!

RAJNA. Eurgh.

THAMANNA. Kinetic?

RAJNA. Too corporate.

SABINA. Sounds like a science class.

PARVIN. I quite like Synergy.

RAJNA. Yeah, but you work at Canary Wharf.

PARVIN. Not for much longer.

RAJNA. How about Matriarchy?

SABINA. Oh please, that makes us sound like grannies.

THAMANNA. Yeah, all toothless.

RAJNA. It's the opposite of patriarchy.

SABINA. Yeah, I know what it means, it's just rubbish.

PARVIN. What about Tigers?

SABINA. Hmm, maybe.

THAMANNA. Yeah, like Bengal Tigers.

SABINA. Isn't that a cricket team?

PARVIN. Yeah, but like, we're kitties at home but out in the wilderness it brings out our wildcat.

SABINA. Nice one, Parv, that is *exactly* the sort of thing. (*Turns to the others*.) Tigers?

THAMANNA. Cool, I can go with that.

SABINA. Raj?

RAJNA. Can it be Tigresses?

SABINA. No.

RAJNA. Why not?

SABINA. It's harder to say.

PARVIN. But tigers do kill men sometimes.

RAJNA. Okay then.

SABINA. Wicked. Do the growl.

They all growl.

Go, Tigers! Do the roar.

They roar.

SABINA (*to audience*). And with that, we were off.

THAMANNA. OH. MY. GOD.

SABINA (*to audience*). Well, almost off.

RAJNA. What?

THAMANNA. I've just thought of something.

SABINA. What?

THAMANNA. Something awful.

PARVIN. What?

THAMANNA. Oh my God, we can't go.

SABINA. Why not?

PARVIN. What is it?

THAMANNA. Man, why didn't I think of this before?

ALL. What – what?!!

THAMANNA. What if… people think we're terrorists?

SABINA. Oh man, what are you on about?

THAMANNA. Think about it! Muslims, backpacks, catching the train to the forest? They might think we're going on a training weekend!

SABINA. What, in How to Catch Heffalumps?

RAJNA. Bring it on! I would take that trial all the way to the European Court. They'll wish they never messed with Rajna Khanom.

SABINA. 'The Heffalump Trial.'

THAMANNA. But we could get flung in jail for, like, for ever!

SABINA. That is one of the dumbest things you've ever said, T.

PARVIN. And you do say quite a lot of dumb things.

THAMANNA. Shut up!

SABINA. I thought you were a copper anyway.

THAMANNA. I'm just a Pretend Copper!

SABINA. Now it comes out.

THAMANNA. To the real ones, we might look dangerous!

SABINA. The most dangerous thing you're carrying, T, is your imagination. Come on, let's go.

(*To audience*.) And with that, we were finally off to the Hundred Acre Wood.

They set off.

RAJNA. Can I lead? Just till we get to the forest.

SABINA. Yeah, okay.

RAJNA. Then it's over to you, Commander.

SABINA *gives* RAJNA *the train map and timetable*.

RAJNA *salutes*.

Right then. DLR to Bank.

SABINA (*to audience*). On the journey, I check my phone.

PARVIN. So many suits.

RAJNA. It's rush hour.

SABINA (*to audience*). Cos I've been getting these messages.

RAJNA. Good timing, Sab.

SABINA (*to audience*). These texts.

THAMANNA. So is Bank, like, one massive bank?

RAJNA. Yeah. No.

SABINA (*to audience*). Anonymous texts.

RAJNA. It's complicated.

SABINA (*to audience*). From a number I don't know.

RAJNA. Northern Line to London Bridge.

SABINA (*to audience*). Messages from a girl.

THAMANNA. Where's the bridge then?

PARVIN. It fell down, didn't it.

THAMANNA. Oh yeah.

SABINA (*to audience*). A girl with allegations.

RAJNA. Mainline to East Croydon.

SABINA (*to audience*). Allegations about my brother.

THAMANNA. Man, this is the furthest east I have ever been.

RAJNA. It's south actually.

THAMANNA. Then why is it called East Croydon?

PARVIN. Good point.

SABINA (*to audience*). I think about telling the others.

> SABINA *is about to speak but* PARVIN *interrupts her.*

PARVIN. Keep your voice down, this is East Croydon. If they hear a Tower Hamlets accent we're dead.

THAMANNA. Really?

SABINA (*to audience*). But then I think again.

RAJNA. Nah, that's only if you're a boy.

THAMANNA. Oh yeah, postcode wars. I think it's disgusting – the Post Office should do something.

RAJNA. Then one more train to East Grinstead.

PARVIN. Wherever that is.

THAMANNA. I told you we was going east.

SABINA (*to audience*). The messages say – they say she's pregnant.

THAMANNA. Be in Bangladesh soon.

SABINA (*to audience*). And that the baby's his. Abdul's. My brother's.

RAJNA. Bangladesh is south-east.

SABINA (*to audience*). But that he doesn't want to know.

RAJNA. Your geography is appalling.

SABINA (*to audience*). And that to cover it up, her family are marrying her off to someone else.

RAJNA. This is it! Everybody off!

THAMANNA (*reading from a sign*). 'East Grinstead.'

PARVIN. Sounds grim.

RAJNA. Sounds dead.

THAMANNA. Aw, it's like a little village, it's cute!

SABINA (*to audience*). I reread the texts to myself.

RAJNA. This way!

SABINA (*to audience*). Again and again and again.

PARVIN. I thought it was this way.

SABINA (*to audience*). Not knowing what to think.

RAJNA. We gotta get a bus.

THAMANNA. Oh man, really?

SABINA (*to audience*). What to feel.

THAMANNA. I swear we're gonna fall off the end of the world, like, any minute.

SABINA (*to audience*). I mean, what does she expect me to do?

RAJNA (*to bus driver*). One please.

SABINA (*to audience*). I don't even know her.

THAMANNA (*to bus driver*). One please.

SABINA (*to audience*). I would wonder if it's even true, but –

PARVIN (*to bus driver*). One please.

SABINA (*to audience*). But –

RAJNA. Sabina?

SABINA (*to audience*). But this isn't the first time it's happened.

RAJNA. Sab?

SABINA (*to bus driver*). One please.

   (*To audience*.) I just wonder who the poor girl is this time.

PARVIN. I feel sick.

RAJNA. That's just buses

SABINA (*to audience*). I did try ringing the number back –

RAJNA. You'll be fine.

SABINA (*to audience*). – but there's never any answer.

RAJNA. This is us! Everybody off!

SABINA (*to audience*). Except for once.

RAJNA. We made it!

PARVIN. Man, this really is the middle of nowhere.

SABINA (*to audience*). But no one spoke –

THAMANNA. Yeah, this has gotta be at least Zone Four.

SABINA (*to audience*). There was just the sound of crying.

RAJNA. Hey, Sabina.

SABINA (*to audience*). Rule Five: Never go camping with a
   burning secret in your pocket. It's like a hot coal – sooner or
   later it'll burn a hole, and fall out onto the ground for
   everyone else to see.

RAJNA. Sabina?

SABINA (*to audience*). And anyone who touches it will only
   get burnt.

RAJNA. Sab?

SABINA. Uh? Oh, yeah, sorry.

RAJNA. You're miles away, girl – where's your head at?

SABINA. Just thinking.

RAJNA. You okay?

SABINA. Yeah, fine.

RAJNA. Good. Well, we're here. Over to you, Captain.

RAJNA *hands* SABINA *the map*.

THAMANNA. There's a campsite!

PARVIN. Ah, wicked, does this mean I can put this weight down?

SABINA. Woah woah woah, no way.

PARVIN. Why not?

SABINA. This is just the start.

PARVIN. The start of what?

RAJNA. Told you she'd get all SAS.

THAMANNA. We've been travelling for days.

SABINA. It's been two hours, T.

THAMANNA. Why can't we stay here?

PARVIN. Hey, this might be the one we stayed at when we was little!

THAMANNA. Oh yeah!

SABINA. That could've been anywhere.

PARVIN. Look, there's showers!

THAMANNA. And a shop!

PARVIN. And a chemical toilet!

THAMANNA. Woohoo!

SABINA. Winnie-the-Pooh did not live on a campsite with showers and a chemical toilet.

THAMANNA. How do you know?

SABINA. Cos he lived in the House at Pooh Corner.

THAMANNA. Exactly – a house.

SABINA. Look, do you wanna do this properly or not?

THAMANNA. Not really.

PARVIN. Yeah, we're here to have fun, not turn into stinky tramps.

THAMANNA. There's boys too, look.

RAJNA. Oh, really? Let's get out of here.

SABINA. Tham, if you don't get out of your comfort zone, how will you ever discover your limits?

THAMANNA. I know my limits: hot showers and chocolate.

RAJNA. I don't like the look of it. All the litter. And someone's already pumping out techno and it's only 7 p.m.

SABINA. Exactly. Come on. We want proper wilderness.

RAJNA. Where's that then?

SABINA. There.

(*To audience*.) And we all turn to face the forest.

THAMANNA. Oh my gosh.

RAJNA. Is that the way?

PARVIN. I'm scared.

SABINA (*to audience*). To be fair, it does look like a solid wall of trees with a pitch-black hole in it.

THAMANNA. I ain't going in there.

PARVIN. Nah, nor me.

RAJNA. It does look a bit dark.

SABINA. Ladies! What did we agree – all or nothing?

RAJNA. All.

PARVIN. All.

THAMANNA. I didn't agree nothing.

SABINA. Then you must have agreed all.

THAMANNA. What?

SABINA. Come on!

PARVIN. Really?

SABINA. Are you Tigers or kitties?

RAJNA. Tigers I spose.

PARVIN. Yeah, Tigers.

THAMANNA. I think I might be a kitty after all.

SABINA. Do the roar!

They roar half-heartedly.

Again!

They roar, not much better.

PARVIN. I got a better idea. Take my hand.

They stand in a circle and hold hands.

Bismillahir Rahmanir Rahim[5].
Thank you Allah for all your blessings.
Forgive all our sins, give us all that is good and keep us
away from all that is bad.[6]

ALL. Amin[7].

SABINA (*to audience*). And with that, we set off into the
woods.
It isn't long before the moaning starts.

PARVIN. Are we there yet?

RAJNA. My feet hurt.

THAMANNA. Eurgh, a massive fly!

The sound of a cuckoo.

Oh my God, what is that?

RAJNA. It's just a bird.

SABINA. A cuckoo.

THAMANNA. A what?

SABINA. A cuckoo – that's the noise it makes.

THAMANNA. What does it mean?

SABINA. You what?

THAMANNA. The noise.

SABINA. It means there's a cuckoo around.

THAMANNA. Does it mean it's hungry?

SABINA. I dunno.

THAMANNA. Does it mean it's gonna start hunting?

SABINA (*holds up her thumb and finger*). Tham, it's about that big.

THAMANNA. So it won't eat us?

SABINA. Only if it thinks you're a worm.

RAJNA. Can we stop now?

SABINA. No.

THAMANNA. Yeah, what about here?

SABINA. Too lumpy.

RAJNA. Oh Sab, why do we have to keep walking?

SABINA. To get where we're going.

RAJNA. And where's that?

SABINA. The end.

THAMANNA. Walking is, like, what you do when your brother's taken the car and all the buses are on strike.

SABINA. Exactly.

THAMANNA. Exactly, it's not natural.

SABINA. Think of it as a workout. Keep those legs slim.

THAMANNA. You sayin I got fat legs?

SABINA (*to audience*). And it's then that we notice: Parvin's gone.

(*To the others.*) Where's Parv?

RAJNA. I dunno.

THAMANNA. Oh, what?

SABINA. Parv?

THAMANNA. Parvin!

SABINA. She was at the back.

RAJNA. Uh-oh.

THAMANNA. Maybe the cockatoo got her!

SABINA. Cuckoo.

THAMANNA. Whatever – it made the noise didn't it and now Parvin's GONE.

SABINA. Parvin!

RAJNA. What are we gonna do?

THAMANNA. Go and look for her, I'll stay here.

SABINA. Why don't *you* go and look for her?

THAMANNA. I ain't going nowhere.

RAJNA. I'll go.

SABINA. Thanks, Raj. Don't go out of sight, yeah.

RAJNA. I won't. Stay there.

THAMANNA. We will.

> RAJNA *takes her pack off and goes*.

> I don't like this.

SABINA. Chill out, it'll be fine. She's probably just – you know.

THAMANNA. Oh. Why didn't she tell us?

SABINA. Maybe it's, you know, a number two.

THAMANNA. Eurgh, I didn't think of that.

> SABINA*'s phone beeps*.

SABINA (*to audience*). And it's then that my phone goes. Another message, from that same number: 'Please help. I'm trapped and I don't know what to do.'

THAMANNA. Who's that?

SABINA. No one.

THAMANNA. Show me.

SABINA. No.

THAMANNA. Is it a boy?

SABINA. No.

THAMANNA. Oh my gosh, it's a boy!

SABINA. No it's not.

THAMANNA. Show me then.

SABINA. No.

THAMANNA. Why not if it's not a boy?

SABINA. Because it's none of your business.

THAMANNA. Alright, don't get stroppy.

    RAJNA *comes back with* PARVIN.

    Parv!

SABINA. Where you been?

RAJNA. She was being sick.

THAMANNA. Oh my God, are you ill?

RAJNA. I think it was the bus. She's fine.

THAMANNA. I forgot – you was always like that on school trips, wasn't you?

PARVIN. Yeah.

THAMANNA. I remember when you sicked up on Mr Dewsbury in Year 7.

PARVIN. Yeah.

THAMANNA. That was rank. Bits of samosa.

SABINA. Is it all out?

PARVIN. I think so.

THAMANNA. Sab said you was having a number two.

SABINA. No I didn't.

THAMANNA. You did.

PARVIN (*covers her mouth*). Stop it.

THAMANNA. Yeah, stop it, you're gonna make her go again!

SABINA. You mentioned it.

THAMANNA. You did.

SABINA. You did.

RAJNA. You alright to carry on?

PARVIN *nods*.

It's getting dark.

SABINA. There's a clearing just up there.

THAMANNA. Man, at last.

RAJNA. That'll do me.

THAMANNA. You want a hand with your bag?

PARVIN. I'm fine.

THAMANNA. Good, I can't manage two anyway.

RAJNA (*looks up*). Oh no, is that rain?

SABINA. Yeah. We'd better hurry up.

They move over to the clearing and start to get the tent things out of their different bags.

(*To audience.*) Rule Six: It's a good idea to split the different parts of the tent between you to distribute the weight. But before you set off, make sure you double check you've brought them all. Especially the little bag with all the

Important Bits in it. The clue's in the name. The Important Bits are called the Important Bits because they're important.

THAMANNA. I ain't got it.

PARVIN. I ain't got it.

SABINA. Well, I ain't.

RAJNA. I've not either.

SABINA. Oh my days. One of us has to have it.

RAJNA *holds up a small blue drawstring bag.*

RAJNA. What's wrong with these ones?

SABINA. That's just the tent pegs. There was another bag just like that.

PARVIN. Uh-oh.

SABINA (*threateningly*). What?

PARVIN. Was it blue?

SABINA. Yeah.

PARVIN. With a little string at the top?

SABINA. Yeah.

PARVIN. Oh no.

RAJNA. What?

THAMANNA. Parvin…

PARVIN. I thought it was your little cousin's Lego.

SABINA. What?!

PARVIN. I stuck it in the cupboard.

ALL. Parvin!

PARVIN. I'm sorry!

THAMANNA. What, so we ain't got no tent?

RAJNA. We've got most of it.

SABINA. Just not the bits we need to actually put it up.

THAMANNA (*to* PARVIN). I don't care if you're marrying my brother, I am gonna kill you with my bare hands right now.

THAMANNA runs after PARVIN.

PARVIN. I'm sorry!

RAJNA. Stop it!

THAMANNA. I'm gonna skin you alive and use that for a tent!

RAJNA. Both of you, stop it!

A huge crash of thunder.

ALL. Oh my GOD!!!

It starts to rain heavily.

THAMANNA. My hair!

RAJNA. My books!

PARVIN. My iPod!

SABINA gets the large flysheets of the tent out of her bag.

SABINA. Come on, we can sling these bits over a tree!

RAJNA. You what?

SABINA. Just help me – get a corner each.

They grab a corner each.

Follow me – up and over!

They pull the largest sheet of the tent over a tree branch.

Pull it down!

They pull it down to form a rough shelter.

Now tie the corners!

RAJNA. To what?

SABINA. Anything!

THAMANNA. It's filthy!

SABINA. Just do it!

They use the strings at each corner of the tent covering to tie the corners to whatever they can find.

Now get under!

They dive under.

Don't forget your bags!

They dive out and get their bags and drag them under.

RAJNA. This is horrible!

THAMANNA. I'm soaked!

PARVIN. I thought it was supposed to be summer!

THAMANNA. Can I kill Parvin now?

SABINA. No one's killing anyone, we're in this together.

More thunder.

ALL. Oh my Goooooood!

THAMANNA. I want to go home!

SABINA. This is all part of coming into the wilderness! We'll get through this!

PARVIN. Give me your hands!

They all hold hands.

Bismillahir Rahmanir Rahim. O Allah, do not let us die by Your anger and do not destroy us with Your punishment, but grant us safety.

ALL. Amin.

The rain eases off a little.

SABINA. It's easing off.

RAJNA. Is it?

PARVIN. It worked!

RAJNA. Alhumdulilah![8]

THAMANNA. Now what?

SABINA *gets a camping stove out of her bag and sets it up.*

RAJNA. It's almost dark.

SABINA. That's just the storm.

RAJNA. It's gone 8 p.m., Sab. I think we're probably here for the night.

THAMANNA. What, without a tent? We'll be eaten alive!

SABINA. What, by cuckoos?

THAMANNA. By whatever.

PARVIN. I wanna go back.

RAJNA. What do you think, Sab?

SABINA. It's harder in the dark. I'm not sure which way.

THAMANNA (*points*). It's that way.

RAJNA (*points a different way*). It's that way.

PARVIN (*points a different way*). It's that way.

RAJNA. Sabina?

SABINA. I… I don't know.

THAMANNA. You're the one with the map!

SABINA. It's gone all soggy.

THAMANNA *gets her phone out.*

THAMANNA. Right, that's it, I'm calling for help.

SABINA. Who you gonna call?

THAMANNA. I dunno, the police.

RAJNA. And how are you gonna tell them where we are?

PARVIN. We're near the… tree?

THAMANNA. Oh my days – I ain't got no signal!

The others check their phones.

SABINA. Me neither.

PARVIN. Me neither.

RAJNA. Nor me.

THAMANNA. Oh man!

RAJNA. What is that all about?

SABINA. It is a bit weird.

THAMANNA. I am really freakin out now.

SABINA. Look, we'll be fine. We've got a stove, Rajna's brought curry.

RAJNA gets it out.

We'll have something to eat and talk about it then.

THAMANNA. We're stuck!

PARVIN. I think I'm going to cry.

SABINA (*to audience*). Rule Seven: Pack your food in decent containers. An ice-cream tub is not a decent container.

RAJNA. Oh. Dear.

The lid has come off the top of the ice-cream container which RAJNA put the curry in and it has spilled all over the inside of her bag. She holds her bag out.

Cold curry anyone?

THAMANNA *and* PARVIN *burst into tears.*

SABINA (*to audience*). And as we sat there feeling sorry for ourselves, soaked to the skin, eating cold curry straight out of the bottom of Rajna's rucksack, and listening to the percussion of the rain, something magical happened.

As SABINA talks, the others gather some nearby firewood and pile it up over the gas stove.

At our lowest point, just when everything seemed against us, we realised that all we had left was each other. But that that was all we needed. Because in each other there was hope. And laughter. And love.

THAMANNA. Hey, I got a joke – why does Tigger smell?

PARVIN. I dunno, why does Tigger smell?

THAMANNA. You'd smell too if you played with Pooh all day.

They all laugh.

RAJNA. Thamanna, that is so childish!

SABINA (*to audience*). So as the rain eased off, we gathered some wood, piled it up on the gas stove, and settled down for the night.

THAMANNA. What now? I'm bored.

SABINA (*to audience*). Rule Eight: Don't play Truth or Dare in the middle of a forest. Seriously, just trust me on that one.

THAMANNA. Let's play Truth or Dare.

PARVIN. Alright.

RAJNA. Go on then.

SABINA. Hmm, I'm not sure that's such a good idea.

RAJNA. Hang on, what can the dare be, all the way out here?

PARVIN. That's a point.

SABINA. I don't wanna get in any more trouble, broken legs or anything like that.

THAMANNA. Truth, then.

PARVIN. That's only half the game.

THAMANNA. We can still play it.

RAJNA. Can we? How?

THAMANNA. Who's been in love?

RAJNA. Oh, no way, I'm not touching that one.

THAMANNA. I have.

PARVIN. Have we started?

SABINA. What, you've been in love?

PARVIN. No way!

THAMANNA. Yes way. I am right now.

RAJNA. Tham, are you serious?

PARVIN. You never told us.

THAMANNA. I'm telling you now.

SABINA. Who is it?

THAMANNA. I can't tell you *that*.

SABINA. Why not?

PARVIN. Yeah, come on.

THAMANNA. Nah, sorry.

SABINA. You can't say that then not tell us!

THAMANNA. I can.

SABINA. You're such a tease.

RAJNA. You clearly wanted to talk about it!

THAMANNA. No I don't!

SABINA. Then why did you bring it up?

THAMANNA. It was a mistake, I shouldn't have said anything.

SABINA. No, no, no – that's it now, you gotta say.

THAMANNA. Or what?

RAJNA. Or we summon the wolves.

THAMANNA. How you gonna do that?

RAJNA. Wolf-whistle, innit.

THAMANNA. That'll never work. Oh man, is that why it's called a wolf-whistle?

RAJNA *wolf-whistles*.

Don't!

SABINA. Nah, we just won't stop going on about it.

THAMANNA. I can't tell you!

SABINA. Who?

THAMANNA. I can't.

PARVIN. Who?

THAMANNA. No!

RAJNA. Who?

THAMANNA. Stop it!

ALL (*chanting*). Who! Who! Who! Who! Who! Who! Who!

THAMANNA. Someone from work!

PARVIN. Who?

SABINA. From the beautician's?

PARVIN. They're all girls.

THAMANNA. No, from the… from the police.

PARVIN. OH MY GOSH! You're in love with a policeman?!

THAMANNA. No, not a policeman!

RAJNA. Who then?!

THAMANNA. Someone else…

PARVIN. A PCSO?

THAMANNA. No.

RAJNA. A fireman?

THAMANNA. Nup.

SABINA. A criminal?

They laugh.

RAJNA. Don't be stupid.

THAMANNA. Well…

RAJNA. Oh my God.

SABINA. What?

RAJNA. Oh my God, you're kidding.

THAMANNA. He's not a criminal exactly.

RAJNA. Thamanna!

THAMANNA. He hasn't gone to trial yet!

RAJNA. You're a police officer!

THAMANNA. Only a pretend one!

RAJNA. Thamanna!

SABINA. How did you meet him?

THAMANNA. It was on this bust.

RAJNA. A drugs bust?

THAMANNA. Sort of. It was more like a squat, illegal occupancy, all that.

RAJNA. Thamanna!

PARVIN. Ssh, I wanna hear this!

RAJNA. You're in love with a junkie?

THAMANNA. He isn't a junkie, he was just there seeing some mates!

SABINA. And you believe him?

THAMANNA. Wrong place, wrong time, it could happen to anyone.

SABINA. Did you have to arrest him?

THAMANNA. Nah, I was just there to observe.

PARVIN. Then what?

THAMANNA. We got talking later. In the cells.

SABINA. Oh my days.

RAJNA. Is he in prison now?

THAMANNA. He's on bail.

RAJNA. You're seeing a junkie squatter, on bail, who you had to arrest?

PARVIN. Is he Bengali?

THAMANNA. Yeah, course.

PARVIN. Oh well, that's something then.

RAJNA. I can't believe you, Tham.

SABINA. I can.

RAJNA. Is this a wind-up?

THAMANNA. No! He's just got these eyes –

SABINA. All-ah[9].

THAMANNA. This stubble –

RAJNA. Stop it!

THAMANNA. And this way he talks to me.

PARVIN. Does he call you 'Officer'?

THAMANNA. Nah, don't be stupid.

SABINA. How is that EVER gonna work out?

RAJNA. You tell us, Miss Agony Aunt.

SABINA. That is a bit out of my league.

THAMANNA. Love finds a way.

RAJNA. But you could get sacked!

THAMANNA. I don't care. I'm in love. Don't tell ANYONE.

SABINA. As if.

RAJNA. Sealed lips.

THAMANNA (*to* PARVIN). Especially you.

PARVIN. Yeah, alright.

THAMANNA. Don't want my bro finding out, he'll kill him.

PARVIN. Salim couldn't kill anyone, he's way too nice.

THAMANNA. My dad then.

PARVIN. Yeah, right. Your family's the most easy-going Bengalis I've ever met.

RAJNA. I found out something recently. But you can't tell anyone either, it's properly confidential.

SABINA. Of course.

THAMANNA. Totally.

PARVIN. You bet.

RAJNA. You know the refuge where I volunteer?

SABINA. The one you won't tell us where it is?

THAMANNA. Yeah, I wonder if it really exists.

RAJNA. Course it exists. It's gotta be a secret, hasn't it, otherwise the husbands go round and take their wives back.

THAMANNA. Yeah, yeah.

RAJNA. Shut up. Anyway, someone turned up there. Someone we used to know.

PARVIN. Oh my God, who?

SABINA. You sure you should be telling us this?

RAJNA. It's not, like, a mate or anything.

THAMANNA. Who, who?

RAJNA. Remember Miss Turner from school?

PARVIN. Oh my God.

THAMANNA. Who pulled Danny Allfield out of the toilet?

RAJNA. Remember how gorgeous she was?

SABINA. Mixed race –

PARVIN. Beautiful smile –

THAMANNA. The sexiest dresses –

RAJNA. Yeah, the boys went mad over her.

PARVIN. Those English classes where she'd read Juliet and they all wanted to do Romeo.

SABINA. Ain't never seen em that into Shakespeare.

RAJNA. And then she got engaged.

THAMANNA. Oh yeah!

SABINA. Boys were gutted.

THAMANNA. He bought her like the massivest ring you've ever seen.

PARVIN. Weren't they gonna hire a castle or something?

RAJNA. Yeah, all that, proper fairy tale it was.

THAMANNA. That was a great summer term. Set us all dreaming. Summer of lurve.

RAJNA. Well, she turned up.

SABINA. No way.

PARVIN. At the refuge?

RAJNA. Yep. Barely recognised her. Covered in bruises, afraid for her life.

THAMANNA. No way.

RAJNA. Covered her face when she saw me. Two black eyes, like this big sad panda.

PARVIN. Poor Miss Turner.

RAJNA. I know, innit. I guess the dreamy fiancé wasn't so dreamy after all.

   Pause.

THAMANNA. You've ruined that summer term for me now.

RAJNA. Sorry.

THAMANNA. I always imagined she went off to live in that castle, like Madonna.

SABINA. Life ain't like that, is it.

THAMANNA. It is for Madonna.

RAJNA. She got divorced.

THAMANNA. Oh yeah.

SABINA (*to audience*). It's then that I bring it up. Cos it's there, inside me, turning round and round like a little razor blade or something.

(*To the others*.) I've been getting these texts.

(*To audience*.) And as I tell them, about the messages, about my brother, about the anonymous pregnant girl, about how I don't know who she is or what to do – they go quiet. Really quiet. Cos this is serious.

THAMANNA. Can we see?

SABINA *shows them her phone*. THAMANNA *and* RAJNA *crowd round to read them, while* PARVIN *sits a short distance away*.

SABINA (*to audience*). Rule Nine: Just because you're outside of the community, doesn't mean the community is outside of you.

THAMANNA. That is deep.

RAJNA. God, yeah.

THAMANNA. What are you gonna do?

SABINA. I don't know.

RAJNA. Who is she?

SABINA. I don't know.

THAMANNA. Someone has to know her.

SABINA (*to audience*). And it's then that we notice. Parvin's crying. Sat there on her own, in floods and floods of tears.

RAJNA. Parv?

THAMANNA. Parvin?

RAJNA. What's the matter?

PARVIN *sobs*.

PARVIN. It's me.

RAJNA. What?

PARVIN. It's me.

Pause.

SABINA (*to audience*). And those two little words sit there in the damp night air. Like a demon screaming our names.

THAMANNA *drops* SABINA*'s phone.*

THAMANNA. Oh God. Oh God. Oh God.

RAJNA. But this means… this means…

SABINA. Parvin?

PARVIN. I'm sorry. I'm so, so sorry. Help me. Please help me.

Small pause.

THAMANNA. You SLUT!

THAMANNA *launches herself at* PARVIN *as if she is going to attack her.*

SABINA *and* RAJNA *hold her back.* PARVIN *scurries further away.*

RAJNA. No – Tham – No!

THAMANNA. My brother! It's my brother!

SABINA. *Your* brother? What about mine?

RAJNA. Stop it, both of you!

THAMANNA. Mine's the one she's marrying!

SABINA. Mine's the babyfather!

THAMANNA. Your brother's a dickhead!

RAJNA. I said STOP IT!

RAJNA *positions herself between* THAMANNA *and* SABINA.

THAMANNA. Around *me* – around *her*! He just can't keep it in his trousers!

RAJNA. Stop it!

SABINA. It's not my fault!

THAMANNA. Your mum's then!

SABINA *moves to attack* THAMANNA. RAJNA *moves to prevent her.*

SABINA. You nasty little –

RAJNA. Don't – Sab – don't!

SABINA. Don't you *dare* start on her!

THAMANNA. Someone should've taught the boy some respect!

RAJNA *physically holds them apart.*

RAJNA. Both of you – stop speaking – NOW!

Pause. PARVIN *has curled up in a ball nearby and is sobbing.*

We don't even know if it's true.

PARVIN. It's true.

RAJNA. Oh Parv.

RAJNA *goes to comfort* PARVIN. *She hesitates to leave* SABINA *and* THAMANNA.

(*To* THAMANNA *and* SABINA.) DON'T hit each other.

THAMANNA *and* SABINA *stand, breathless.*

RAJNA *goes to* PARVIN. PARVIN *clutches her.*

Oh Parvin. Come on, it's alright. It's alright. Ssh ssh ssh.

THAMANNA. My family. Oh God, my family.

SABINA (*to* PARVIN). You were seeing my brother?

THAMANNA. I feel sick.

SABINA. Parvin, my brother? Behind my back?

PARVIN *continues to cry.* RAJNA *continues to hold her.*

RAJNA. Not now, Sabina.

SABINA. Why not? She needs to face up to what she's done!

RAJNA. Leave her alone.

SABINA. She should have left my brother alone!

THAMANNA. And mine!

PARVIN. It takes two, alright!

THAMANNA. Well, now there's three involved!

RAJNA. Parvin, you don't have to do this now.

SABINA. We don't even know if she's telling the truth!

PARVIN. Why would I lie?

SABINA. I don't know! But you went to the trouble of buying a new SIM to text me! What was that all about?!

PARVIN. I didn't know what else to do! I can't talk to anyone – tell *anyone*. It's killing me.

THAMANNA. But you'd have duped my brother into marrying you.

PARVIN. No.

THAMANNA. Then what? Pretended it was his?

PARVIN. No –

THAMANNA. You nasty piece of work.

RAJNA. Thamanna –

THAMANNA. Anyone'd think butter wouldn't melt, but you had this all mapped out, didn't you?

PARVIN. It was my parents!

THAMANNA. Don't blame them!

PARVIN. You know what they can be like!

SABINA. Does Abdul know?

PARVIN. Know what?

SABINA. About this, of course! You. It.

PARVIN. Yeah.

SABINA. What did he say?

PARVIN. He went mental, Sab. I've never seen him like that before.

THAMANNA. I have. (*To* SABINA.) That time with your mum.

SABINA. Shut up, Tham.

PARVIN. Yeah, well, you'll both know then. He even raised his fist.

RAJNA. To you?

PARVIN nods.

Even once he knew you were –

PARVIN. Yeah.

RAJNA. Oh God.

THAMANNA. You have to go back to him.

RAJNA. What?

PARVIN. No!

THAMANNA. Tell him to do the right thing.

PARVIN. He won't. I've tried.

THAMANNA (*to* SABINA). Won't he?

Small pause.

Sab? Won't he?

SABINA (*quietly*). This isn't the first time.

PARVIN. What?

RAJNA. Oh, the little –

THAMANNA. I told you – I bloody told you, didn't I?

RAJNA. Thamanna –

THAMANNA. Boy's out of control – and whose fault is that?

SABINA. Don't start.

RAJNA. Tham, please.

PARVIN. Who was it before?

SABINA. It doesn't matter.

PARVIN. Yeah, it does!

SABINA. No one we know! Alright? He denied it then and all.

RAJNA. What happened?

SABINA. She had an abortion.

PARVIN. I'm gonna be sick.

THAMANNA. Oh GOD!

THAMANNA *kicks a bag, hard*.

RAJNA. Calm down! We all just need to – to stay calm.

SABINA. Do you love him?

PARVIN. Which one?

THAMANNA / SABINA. Whichever!

PARVIN. Abdul? I thought I did. But not now. Salim? He's lovely –

THAMANNA. Forget it.

PARVIN. What?

THAMANNA. No way you're marrying him!

RAJNA. Thamanna –

THAMANNA. No way you're bringing that – (*Points to PARVIN's belly.*) thing, into our house.

RAJNA. That is an innocent baby!

THAMANNA. It stinks of your shame!

RAJNA. Stop this!

SABINA. Yeah, I'm its auntie!

THAMANNA (*to PARVIN*). You can keep it! Ain't no way I'll let it stink up my family and all!

RAJNA (*to* THAMANNA). You can't take this stuff back!

Pause.

SABINA (*to* PARVIN). How long were you seeing him?

RAJNA. I really don't think we should talk about this now.

SABINA. Parv? How long?

RAJNA. I mean it.

PARVIN. A few months.

RAJNA. Please.

PARVIN. He was lovely at first.

SABINA. He always is.

RAJNA. I hate to see us like this. We're best friends.

THAMANNA. Yeah, well, maybe not any more.

SABINA. You what?

RAJNA. You don't mean that.

PARVIN. Thamanna, no –

RAJNA (*to* PARVIN). It's alright, she doesn't mean it.

THAMANNA. Don't I?

RAJNA. Guys, let's not throw everything away here. Alright? What we've got is too precious.

SABINA. Well, maybe she should've thought of that before she did what she did.

PARVIN. I'm begging you, all of you, please. You have to keep this quiet.

THAMANNA. Why? So you can trap my brother?

PARVIN. For the sake of the baby! Why should it have to suffer for my mistakes?

THAMANNA. Why should Salim?!

SABINA. Why should I?

RAJNA. Alright, enough.

PARVIN. We could bring it up together, as aunties, guarding its secret against the rest of –

THAMANNA. No way.

RAJNA. Please stop this –

PARVIN. Sisters, then. Sharing its burden.

THAMANNA. You're no sister of mine.

RAJNA. This is tearing us apart!

PARVIN. Look, I know I did wrong, okay?! I know it. But what I need from you now is help, not hate. Because I've got the rest of my life to hate myself for it. Maybe one day this baby can know the truth, but not now, not yet. Until then, we've gotta carry this thing for it. Allow it a childhood at the very least.

SABINA. That is so cowardly.

PARVIN. What?

RAJNA. Leave it, Sab.

SABINA. That is like something –

RAJNA. Leave it!

SABINA. – like something *Piglet* would come out with!

PARVIN. This is my life, okay! Not a stupid story!

RAJNA. Exactly – Winnie-the-Pooh is pathetic!

SABINA. Excuse me?

RAJNA. The stupid Pooh characters are all boys – boys and their stupid failings! Tigger's got Attention Deficit Disorder, Eeyore's a manic depressive, Pooh has – has some bloody eating disorder and Rabbit's obsessive compulsive! Even Owl has dyslexia! The only female character is Kanga and she's an overprotective mother – how predictable is that? It's a stupid story about stupid little boys, the kind that are messing up our lives right now.

SABINA (*to audience*). Rule Ten: never debate children's
      stories with a feminist academic.
      You'll never win.

RAJNA. We're best friends, remember? Why should we let men
      come between us? They can bring out the best, but they can
      also destroy us. Well, I won't let them. I won't let them.

There is a noise in the darkness, just out of sight.

THAMANNA. Oh my God.

RAJNA. What was that?

SABINA. Did you hear that?

RAJNA. Something's there.

THAMANNA. Go away!

RAJNA. We heard you!

THAMANNA. We've got knives!

RAJNA. Have we? I haven't.

      SABINA *grabs a handful of tent pegs and hands them one
      each.*

SABINA. Take this.

      They hold them like weapons.

      A little GIRL *appears. She is soaked to the skin and has a
      strange, shell-shocked air about her.*

THAMANNA. Oh my God.

PARVIN. Oh my God.

THAMANNA. What the hell is that?

SABINA. Chill out, it's just a kid.

RAJNA. Where did *she* come from?

SABINA. She's soaked.

RAJNA. Where did you come from?

SABINA. What's your name?

The GIRL *doesn't speak, she just stands there*. RAJNA *goes to her.*

RAJNA. Hey, hey, what's the matter?

SABINA. Get her under the tent.

THAMANNA. No.

SABINA. What?

THAMANNA. This is weird.

RAJNA. Don't be stupid.

THAMANNA. This is really weird.

SABINA. There must be a family nearby, she's lost.

THAMANNA. I don't like this.

SABINA. She's lost. Are you lost?

RAJNA. She's shivering.

SABINA. Put her by the fire. (*Calling off.*) Hello! Is anyone out there?

RAJNA (*calling off*). Hello? We've got your little girl!

THAMANNA. Oh my God, this is really freaking me out.

SABINA. She'll be from the campsite or somewhere.

THAMANNA. That's miles away!

RAJNA. Stop it, you're scaring her. Sweetheart, come and sit down.

PARVIN. I'm – I'm not sure about this either.

SABINA. She's just a little kid.

PARVIN. What if she's a ghost?

THAMANNA. Yeah!

RAJNA. Oh, leave it out, does she look like a ghost?

SABINA. Looks real to me.

THAMANNA. Don't touch her!

RAJNA. Oh, don't be ridiculous. She's cold.

THAMANNA. Course she's cold, she's a jinn[10] or something!

SABINA. Thamanna, I really think you should shut up.

RAJNA. So do I. (*To the* GIRL.) Come near the fire. Come on. You're safe now.

THAMANNA. Why doesn't she speak?

RAJNA. Probably cos she's terrified of you.

PARVIN. Maybe she doesn't speak English. She does look Bengali.

THAMANNA. What is a Bengali doing all the way out here?

SABINA. We're here, aren't we?

RAJNA. Do you speak English?

THAMANNA. What if she possesses us?

RAJNA. Go over there, and shut up. We'll deal with this.

> THAMANNA *goes a short distance away and starts chanting, reciting duas under her breath.*

Tumi Bangla matho ni?[11]

SABINA. Tumar naam kitha?[12]

RAJNA. Maybe she's lost her voice.

PARVIN. Maybe she's one of those wild children that was raised by wolves or something.

SABINA. No, too clean.

RAJNA. Too well dressed.

PARVIN. Maybe she only speaks wolf.

> *The* GIRL *sits by the fire and puts her hands out.*

RAJNA. That's it, warm yourself up.

SABINA. This is pretty weird, Raj.

RAJNA. Don't you freak out as well.

SABINA. I mean, no words, no expressions –

RAJNA. Yeah, well, maybe something awful's happened to her.

Small pause.

Get a blanket, she's shivering.

PARVIN *gets one and they wrap it round the* GIRL*'s shoulders.*

(*Of the chanting.*) Thamanna, would you stop that?

THAMANNA. It's for protection.

SABINA. You're scaring her.

RAJNA. We don't need protecting, she's a little girl.

THAMANNA. You don't know what she is.

SABINA. You're freaking everyone out.

RAJNA. She's a normal little girl, okay? I can see her, touch her, look.

RAJNA *strokes the* GIRL*'s hair.*

Soaking. Get a towel. Thamanna – get a towel.

THAMANNA *does so.*

SABINA. How old do you reckon she is?

RAJNA. I don't know. Seven? Eight?

SABINA. Man, this is pretty freaky. Where the hell could she have come from?

RAJNA (*calling into the forest*). Hello! She's over here!

They listen.

Nothing. Can you see any torches?

SABINA. No.

PARVIN. Nah.

SABINA. Shit.

RAJNA. Don't swear in front of her.

SABINA. Sorry. Maybe we should, erm…

RAJNA. What?

SABINA. I don't know. Go out and look?

RAJNA. Not in the dark. We'd lose you and all.

THAMANNA brings the towel.

THAMANNA. Well, what are we gonna do then?

RAJNA. Look after her. What else can we do? You can dry her hair for a start.

THAMANNA does so. RAJNA realises the GIRL*'s clothes are soaked too.*

Oh look, her clothes and everything. Sab, you got any dry clothes?

SABINA. Sure.

SABINA gets some.

PARVIN. If only she'd speak.

Takes her by both hands.

What is your name?

No answer.

Where have you come from?

SABINA has brought dry clothes.

SABINA. Maybe she's hypothermic or something.

PARVIN. What does that mean?

SABINA. Dangerously cold.

THAMANNA. You mean like a ghost?

SABINA. No, like a human. (*Of the clothes.*) Here, give us a hand, would you.

They change the GIRL *into dry clothes. The clothes are far too big for her.*

RAJNA. Someone's got to be looking for her, even if they don't realise she's gone yet.

PARVIN. Maybe she's asleep.

SABINA. How do you mean?

PARVIN. Like, maybe she sleepwalked out of her tent.

SABINA. Maybe.

PARVIN. I used to do that when I was little. Ended up in the lift once, Dad found me just in time.

THAMANNA. Don't tell me, that's how you ended up in Abdul's bed, right?

Tense pause.

RAJNA (*with force*). Not now. Okay? Not. Now.

THAMANNA *and* PARVIN *back down.*

SABINA *waves her hand in front of the* GIRL's *face.*

SABINA. Hello – are you awake?

The GIRL *looks at her.*

Seems awake.

RAJNA. Has anyone got a phone signal yet?

They all check.

SABINA. Nope.

PARVIN. Nup.

THAMANNA. Nah.

RAJNA. Me neither.

SABINA. What are we gonna do?

RAJNA (*sighs and checks her watch*). It's late. Past *her* bedtime anyway. One of us should stay up with her. In case someone comes looking.

SABINA. What about the rest of us?

RAJNA (*shrugs*). Get some sleep.

THAMANNA. We were in the middle of a really important conversation, actually.

RAJNA. Yeah, well, something more important's come up, hasn't it? More important than us. Let's get a bed ready for her, yeah? Have we got any dry blankets?

THAMANNA. Everything's soaked.

PARVIN. Mine too.

SABINA. I got one I wrapped in plastic.

RAJNA. Get it out.

THAMANNA. What about...

SABINA / RAJNA / PARVIN. What?

THAMANNA. Nothing. You're right. She's more important, innit.

They all pitch in, setting up a bed for the GIRL *with the only dry things they have.*

RAJNA (*to the* GIRL). Just sit there, my darling, we'll look after you.

THAMANNA. Poor little thing. She looks so scared.

RAJNA. Thamanna, sing her one of your songs or something.

THAMANNA *starts to sing as they set up the bed.*[13]

When the bed is ready they settle the GIRL *down and tuck her in.*

SABINA *takes out her Winnie-the-Pooh book.*

Night-night, sweetheart.

RAJNA *kisses her forehead.*

(*To the others.*) Say goodnight, yeah.

They each say goodnight to the child.

SABINA. Night-night.

PARVIN. Night-night.

THAMANNA. Night-night.

RAJNA. Don't be scared, yeah.

THAMANNA (*to the* GIRL). I'm – I'm sorry about what I said earlier. We'll look after you. I promise.

RAJNA. Thanks, T. Who's gonna stay up with her?

SABINA. I'll do it. (*Holds up book*.) Got stories and everything.

RAJNA. Cool, thanks, Sab. Give us a nudge if you get sleepy.

PARVIN. Yeah, we'll take it in turns.

THAMANNA. Yeah, and me.

SABINA. Thanks, guys.

(*To audience*.) And just like that, the most painful night of our lives came to the weirdest end. I sat there and looked in the girl's eyes, heavy now from sleep. But they weren't giving nothing away. So I opened up the book, and lulled her tales with from the Hundred Acre Wood.

From Chapter Ten, where they go to the Enchanted Place. The place where Christopher Robin tells Pooh that soon, he won't be allowed to do nothing any more. Where he asks Pooh to promise to never forget about him, not even when he is one hundred, and Pooh is ninety-nine.

The part where Christopher Robin looks out at the world, and asks Pooh to understand, but Pooh doesn't, because he can't, because he's just a bear. So Christopher Robin says 'Never mind,' and then 'Come on!', and Pooh says 'Where to?' and Christopher Robin says 'Anywhere.'

The part where they go off together, and we leave them there, playing… for ever… in the Enchanted Place.

The part that always made me sad, though I never understood why.

The very end of all the stories. Where they have to say goodbye.

The GIRL *is fast asleep, along with* THAMANNA, RAJNA *and* PARVIN.

SABINA *closes the book. The storm and rain have completely stopped now and it is a calm, clear night.*

Rule Eleven: The storm will always end. It might not seem like it at the time, but it will. Always.

SABINA *lies down and goes to sleep.*

The lights change – it is morning. The sun is streaming through the trees.

PARVIN *is the first to wake up and look around. The* GIRL *has gone.*

PARVIN. Oh my God. Wake up. Wake up!

RAJNA. What?

PARVIN. She's gone!

RAJNA. Who?

PARVIN. The girl!

RAJNA. Oh my God. Guys, wake up.

THAMANNA. Urrrh.

RAJNA. Look.

RAJNA *indicates the bed where the* GIRL *was sleeping. It is empty.*

SABINA. What the hell –

RAJNA. Where did she go?

PARVIN. I don't know!

SABINA. She must be around here somewhere.

PARVIN (*calling off*). Hello!

RAJNA (*calling off*). Little girl! Man, we don't even know her name!

PARVIN (*calling off*). Hello!

SABINA. Maybe her parents came and got her.

THAMANNA. What's going on?

RAJNA. Get up, Grandma.

THAMANNA. What?

RAJNA. The kid's gone. Look.

> RAJNA *goes through the* GIRL*'s bed. There are just* SABINA*'s dry clothes lying there, which the* GIRL *was wearing.*

SABINA. My clothes.

THAMANNA. This is a dream, this has gotta be a dream.

SABINA. Maybe she's gone for a wee or something.

PARVIN. Come back!

RAJNA. Why would she have taken off your clothes?

SABINA. I – I don't know.

PARVIN. Someone must have come and got her, and – and –

RAJNA. And what?

PARVIN. And seen what she was wearing and left it!

RAJNA. Why would they do that?

THAMANNA. Oh God. Oh God. She was a ghost.

SABINA. Oh, shut up.

THAMANNA. I told you she was a ghost!

RAJNA. We all saw her, didn't we? Touched her.

THAMANNA. That doesn't mean anything!

PARVIN. Little girl! Come back!

SABINA. Teek aseh! Tumi okhon ayta pharbai![14]

THAMANNA. Maybe she went inside one of us.

RAJNA. Don't be silly.

THAMANNA. Like a jinn.

SABINA. It is like she disappeared.

PARVIN. I'm scared.

RAJNA. You're always scared.

PARVIN. Maybe someone came and stole her.

SABINA. Who would do that?

PARVIN. I don't know, a pervert!

THAMANNA. Maybe she got eaten by wolves.

PARVIN. That's a point.

SABINA. Then where's the blood?

RAJNA. This is ridiculous, she's got to be around here somewhere. Check.

They check the rest of their camp.

SABINA. Nothing.

PARVIN. No one.

THAMANNA. Kichunai[15].

RAJNA. That's – impossible.

SABINA. What are we gonna do?

PARVIN. We were supposed to be looking after her.

RAJNA. Sab, did you go to sleep?

SABINA. I don't remember.

THAMANNA. You must've.

RAJNA. We were gonna take it in turns!

SABINA. I'm sorry!

PARVIN. Look, blaming each other is not helpful.

RAJNA. Yeah, you're right. I'm sorry.

PARVIN. Any one of us could have done it.

THAMANNA. Yeah, sorry, Sab.

PARVIN. Maybe she made you go to sleep, like a spell.

RAJNA. Look, we have to assume she's real.

SABINA. Rajna's right.

RAJNA. Which means we have to tell someone.

THAMANNA. Who's gonna believe us?

RAJNA. Everyone – we all saw her. She might've wandered off, and, and, hurt herself.

SABINA. That's true – got lost.

RAJNA. Passed out.

THAMANNA. All on her own.

PARVIN. Cold and scared.

SABINA. Poor little thing.

THAMANNA. I've got a phone signal!

SABINA. Really?

PARVIN. Me too!

RAJNA. Alhumdulilah, at last. Call the police.

THAMANNA. I'm already there.

THAMANNA *calls*.

RAJNA. Pack this place up, we need to get to a main road.

They pack up the camp, quickly. As they do so a police siren sounds and a blue light begins to flash.

SABINA (*to audience*). That was it, the whole rest of the day. Blue lights, police cars, uniforms, statements, descriptions, questions, and cups of sweet tea. Whatever you think of the police, they don't half move when it's a missing kid.

RAJNA. It was about half nine.

PARVIN. Ten.

THAMANNA. At least midnight.

SABINA. It was dark.

RAJNA. About seven years old?

PARVIN. Asian – Bengali, I think.

THAMANNA. Long hair.

SABINA. A colourful dress.

RAJNA. Flowers.

PARVIN. Stripes.

THAMANNA. I can't remember.

SABINA. Caught in the storm.

RAJNA. Dried her off.

PARVIN. Settled her down.

THAMANNA. Thought about looking for her parents, but –

SABINA. But –

RAJNA. But –

PARVIN. It was dark.

THAMANNA. We had the fire.

SABINA. Thought we'd wait.

RAJNA. Dried her hair.

PARVIN. Gave her clothes.

THAMANNA. Sang her a song.

SABINA. Didn't speak once.

RAJNA. I swear.

PARVIN. Not a word.

THAMANNA. Man, it was weird.

SABINA. Really freaked us out.

RAJNA. Me? I'm a student.

PARVIN. Receptionist.

THAMANNA. Beautician.

SABINA. Writer – journalist – sort of. Why do you need to know all this?

RAJNA. I don't like what you're implying.

PARVIN. None of us had a signal.

THAMANNA. Like, *totally* lost.

SABINA. Soaked through.

RAJNA. Didn't think –

PARVIN. Didn't know –

THAMANNA. Didn't want –

SABINA. Didn't realise –

They all take a deep breath.

RAJNA. We'd had an argument.

PARVIN. Something… came up.

THAMANNA. It was… difficult, alright?

SABINA. Difficult to explain, but –

RAJNA. Look, can we stop for a minute?

PARVIN. I'd like to see my friends.

THAMANNA. Are we in trouble?

SABINA. Am I under arrest?

RAJNA. Do we need a lawyer here?

PARVIN. We did everything we could.

THAMANNA. Looked after her.

SABINA. Did the right thing.

RAJNA. Like sisters.

PARVIN. Like aunties.

THAMANNA. Like adults.

ALL. Is that a crime?

*The camp has been cleared and the friends are alone. They
stand looking at each other.*

RAJNA. You alright?

PARVIN. Yeah.

THAMANNA. Yeah.

SABINA. Yeah.

A TV flicks on.

(*To audience.*) That night, it was on the news.

PARVIN. How did the news find out?

RAJNA. They pay the police, innit.

THAMANNA. Serious? I gotta get me some of that.

RAJNA. They won't let you be police any more. Not after this.

SABINA (*to audience, of the TV pictures*). And there it is.
Ashdown Forest, swarming with coppers. Helicopters,
photofits, alerts at all the airports. But nothing, not even foot-
prints. But the weirdest thing out of all these weird things –
no one, not anywhere in the whole UK, had even reported a
little girl missing.

RAJNA. This is –

PARVIN. This is –

THAMANNA. This is –

SABINA. Yeah. I know.

RAJNA (*quietly*). What the hell happened to us out there?

PARVIN. Don't.

SABINA (*to audience*). Then, the journalists started.

A doorbell rings.

RAJNA. Go away.

PARVIN. No comment.

THAMANNA. We ain't talking.

SABINA. Leave us alone.

Their phones ring. They each answer them.

RAJNA. I thought I told you.

PARVIN. We have nothing to add.

THAMANNA. I said no comment.

SABINA. How did you get this number?

RAJNA. How *dare* you?

PARVIN. Of course it's true!

THAMANNA. Oh my gosh, how much? Er…

RAJNA takes THAMANNA*'s phone from her, hangs it up.*

RAJNA. No!

SABINA (*to audience*). But none of it was worse than our families.

PARVIN. Amma[16] –

THAMANNA. Abba[17] –

SABINA. Sasi[18] –

RAJNA. Nani[19] –

PARVIN. I swear.

THAMANNA. We ain't kids.

SABINA. You have to believe me.

RAJNA. Get a Qur'an if you like.

PARVIN. The community understands.

THAMANNA. What's shameful?

SABINA. We did the right thing.

RAJNA. What would you have done?

PARVIN. Oh, please.

THAMANNA. Gimme a break.

SABINA. How old am I?

RAJNA. That was in Year 8!

SABINA (*to audience*). Rule Twelve: Stick together. In the great outdoors, there isn't a single situation you'll find yourself in where you'd be better off alone.

They come back together.

THAMANNA. Alright.

SABINA. Not really.

RAJNA. Family?

PARVIN. Innit.

THAMANNA. Yours too?

SABINA. Yeah.

RAJNA. And mine.

PARVIN. My head hurts.

Pause.

Guys… are we going mad?

SABINA. No.

THAMANNA. Course not.

RAJNA. We all saw her, touched her.

PARVIN. Yeah?

ALL. Yeah.

RAJNA. Whatever anyone says. We know the truth.

They take each other's hands.

PARVIN. You're my sanity, you lot.

THAMANNA. Mine too.

SABINA. We gotta stick together.

RAJNA. Yeah, we'll get through this. We will.

PARVIN *starts to say a prayer for them all but it fades into just mouthing it as* SABINA *talks to us*.

PARVIN. Bismillahir Rahmanir Rahim…

SABINA (*to audience*). But all of us with hearts like lead. A wrecking ball inside us all. Knowing there was still this thing – hanging.

The prayer ends.

ALL. *Amin*.

PARVIN *cries*.

RAJNA. Oh Parv.

SABINA. Don't cry.

THAMANNA. We're here.

PARVIN. Maybe it was – you know.

THAMANNA. What?

PARVIN. A sign.

THAMANNA. From who?

PARVIN. I dunno. God.

THAMANNA. You'd think He'd be a bit clearer, wouldn't you?

SABINA. Well, we do still have a problem here.

PARVIN. Have you told anyone?

RAJNA. No.

SABINA. Course not.

THAMANNA. Me neither.

RAJNA. Then it's all to play for.

PARVIN. It isn't a game!

RAJNA. I'm not saying that.

THAMANNA. Don't be so –

PARVIN. What?

THAMANNA. Touchy. Childish.

Small pause.

PARVIN. Alright. I know. I'm sorry.

Small pause.

RAJNA. The way I see it, we got four options. But whichever one we choose, we gotta choose quick. (*Points at* PARVIN*'s belly.*) Ticking clock over there.

SABINA. Go on.

RAJNA. Okay, it's like this. Option One: Stick to the plan.

THAMANNA. What?

SABINA. No way.

PARVIN. You mean go through with the wedding?

THAMANNA. Forget it.

RAJNA. Let me finish. You've got your sisters to think about, Parv.

THAMANNA. I've got my brother to think about!

SABINA. Please, Tham, let her finish.

THAMANNA. But he's completely innocent in all this!

RAJNA. Look, we have to be adults about this. This affects four lives for ever – yours, Salim's, Abdul's, and Sabina's.

PARVIN. And the baby's.

RAJNA. Of course, five. So this is the biggest decision you'll ever make. It's a mess.

PARVIN. I'm so sorry.

RAJNA. This isn't about being sorry. It's about being calm. Reasonable. Okay?

PARVIN. Okay.

SABINA. Okay.

THAMANNA. Okay.

RAJNA. So, your sisters. If this gets out, it could ruin their own chances of marriage.

PARVIN. I know.

RAJNA. The gossip, the association, all that. And they haven't even done anything.

THAMANNA. Neither has Salim.

RAJNA. I know. And that's the other thing. (*To* PARVIN.) If you marry him, you'd have to live with that lie for ever.

SABINA. So would I. The secret auntie.

RAJNA. That's right. There's also the timing.

PARVIN. How do you mean?

RAJNA. Well, how far gone are you?

PARVIN. About six weeks.

RAJNA. Right. So how are you gonna explain a healthy baby arriving after seven or eight months rather than nine?

PARVIN. I don't know.

SABINA. I'd be denying my brother too.

THAMANNA. Denying him what?

SABINA. Access, fatherhood.

RAJNA. There is that.

THAMANNA. He doesn't deserve it.

SABINA. Alright, he might not be mature enough to want it now, but one day, he might. And who are we to make that decision for him?

RAJNA. That's true.

THAMANNA. I couldn't do it to Salim.

RAJNA. Well, that's important. Because you'd have to live with this every day. In your house. In your life.

THAMANNA. Oh God.

PARVIN (*to* THAMANNA). And if we ever fell out, if I ever upset you, or – or –

RAJNA. Don't even go there.

Pause.

SABINA. What's number Two?

RAJNA. Number Two is: We confront Abdul.

PARVIN. Oh, what?

RAJNA. Together. Make him face what he's done. Make him do the right thing.

PARVIN. Force him to marry me?

SABINA. Oh my God.

PARVIN. And how would that work?

THAMANNA. I'd threaten him with my stilettos. Actually, he might quite like that.

SABINA. Oh, please.

RAJNA. Tham, that's really not helpful.

THAMANNA. Sorry. How then?

RAJNA. I don't know. Appeal to his better nature?

THAMANNA. Does he even have one? Sorry, Sab.

PARVIN. I have actually tried that, you know.

RAJNA. Yeah, but on your own. You've got us now. We're a force to be reckoned with.

PARVIN. He'll deny it's his. Say I slept around, whatever. It'd get out of control. He might even... you know.

RAJNA. Parv, I wouldn't let him touch a hair on your head.

THAMANNA. Nah, nor me. I'm sharpening my shoes already.

RAJNA. Sabina?

SABINA. I... I don't think it's an option.

THAMANNA. Why?

SABINA. It's just not, alright?

RAJNA. Come on, you have to be part of this.

Pause.

SABINA. He's been arrested again.

RAJNA. Oh no. What for?

SABINA. I don't know. Violent something or other. He's probably going down this time.

THAMANNA. All-ah.

RAJNA. I'm sorry to hear that.

SABINA. Even if he wasn't… I'm not sure I'd want you to, Parv.

PARVIN. Why not?

SABINA. I… I love you too much.

PARVIN. Oh, Sab.

SABINA. I mean, I love him too, but… he's lost. The pain of it all, it's killing my mum right now. And you'd get that. All of it. As his wife. I couldn't do that to you.

PARVIN *hugs* SABINA.

What sort of marriage would it be? For you, my best mate.

PARVIN. Stop it, I'm gonna cry.

SABINA. Don't cry.

PARVIN. I love you so much.

RAJNA. Oh guys.

PARVIN (*to* RAJNA). And you.

RAJNA *joins their hug. Only* THAMANNA *is left out.*

RAJNA. Sab's right. At the refuge, we pick up the pieces of those marriages every day.

SABINA. And the baby. The resentment. Poor little thing.

PARVIN. I don't even wanna think about that.

They are all about to cry.

RAJNA. Oh!

SABINA. Oh!

PARVIN. I know!

They hold each other close. PARVIN *notices* THAMANNA *is left out.*

T?

THAMANNA. What?

PARVIN. You gonna join us?

No response. They break out of the hug.

That's okay. I get it. I do.

Small pause.

RAJNA. Come on, we got two more options.

They wipe their eyes and pull themselves together.

Option Three: Don't marry either brother.

PARVIN. And what?

RAJNA. And raise the baby alone.

SABINA. Serious?

RAJNA. Why not? We'd rally round you.

SABINA. My cousin's friend did that.

RAJNA. How she's doing?

SABINA. No one knows. Never heard from her, never saw her again.

PARVIN. Exactly. It's a death wish.

RAJNA. Oh, come on, that's a bit melodramatic.

PARVIN. I'd have to move out of Tower Hamlets.

RAJNA. Plenty of people do that.

PARVIN. Yeah, if they get married. On my own I'd have to
   move to Newham or somewhere, live alone in, like, the nas-
   tiest council flat ever, on benefits for the rest of my life.

RAJNA. Why?

PARVIN. Well, how am I gonna work with a baby and no
   husband?

RAJNA. We'd help.

PARVIN. How? Babysitting once a week?

RAJNA. I mean financially. We'd be your husband.

SABINA. What, give her money?

RAJNA. Why not? We've all got careers and no families ourselves yet.

PARVIN. Yeah, but how long is that gonna last? Are you always
   gonna be there for me?

RAJNA. I would.

PARVIN. And what about when your own life takes over,
   Rajna? Your own husband and kids? Or when work means
   you have to move to Scotland or something?

RAJNA. There's your own family too.

SABINA. Oh, who's being immature now?

RAJNA. Why?

SABINA. You know how it works. If Parvin goes it alone, she'd
   be cut off for ever. They isolate you like some rabid dog, so
   you don't contaminate no one else.

RAJNA. It isn't always like that!

SABINA. Oh, come on, this is Parvin's parents we're talking
   about.

PARVIN. She's right, it would be with my lot. If I made a fuss,
   went against what they've arranged –

SABINA. Exactly. No more mehndis, weddings, birthdays, even
   funerals. Imagine if her mum died – she couldn't even go.

RAJNA. I think that's going a bit far, Sab.

SABINA. Is it? No phone calls, nothing. Not even texts.

RAJNA. Always the drama queen with you, isn't it?

PARVIN. We can't all have families like yours, Rajna.

Pause.

RAJNA. Alright. Then the final option.

PARVIN. What?

RAJNA. Get rid of it.

PARVIN. No way.

THAMANNA. An abortion?

SABINA. Forget it.

RAJNA. Who'd have to know?

THAMANNA / SABINA / PARVIN. We would.

PARVIN. I would. I couldn't live with that. This is a child's life, a gift from Allah.

THAMANNA. True say.

PARVIN. You can't reject it.

Pause.

RAJNA. Well. That's that then.

THAMANNA *kicks something.*

THAMANNA. Man! This is, like, the hardest EVER question on *Who Wants to Be a Millionaire*!

SABINA. Except there's no right answer.

PARVIN. Can we ask the audience?

RAJNA. I wish we could. But it's just us.

PARVIN. Phone a friend then.

RAJNA. You are. We're right here.

SABINA. If you were to go fifty-fifty I'd say no abortion and no going it alone.

THAMANNA. So it's Abdul or Salim.

RAJNA. Why does it have to involve a man?

PARVIN. Come on, Raj. I thought we were being grown-ups here.

RAJNA. We are.

PARVIN. Because a baby needs a dad, that's why.

Pause.

SABINA. Oh, why did you do it, Parv?

PARVIN. I'm sorry. It was weird. I wanted to and didn't want to at the same time. Like this war inside me. And I lost. I gave in to evil, and now this is my punishment.

RAJNA. You're not evil, you're human.

PARVIN. But you're all being punished with me, that's what I can't live with.

RAJNA. We'll cope. It's you we've got to worry about.

PARVIN. Oh, God forgive me!

RAJNA. If it's asked from the heart, Inshallah[20], He will.

PARVIN. And you too?

SABINA. Oh, of course we do.

PARVIN. All of you.

RAJNA. Of course.

PARVIN. Thamanna?

THAMANNA. What?

PARVIN. Forgive me. Please.

Pause.

And I'll forgive you.

THAMANNA. What for?

PARVIN. For tearing my heart out, in that forest.

RAJNA. It's true, T. You said some… things.

THAMANNA. Did I?

SABINA. Yeah.

RAJNA. Broke all our hearts that night.

Pause. THAMANNA *looks from one to the other. A moment, and then she puts her arms around* PARVIN.

RAJNA *smiles at* SABINA.

Alhumdulilah.

PARVIN *cries*.

PARVIN. Oh, it's such a mess! And you're all being so nice!

THAMANNA (*quietly*). What are friends for?

RAJNA. Good girl, T.

SABINA. Thank you.

THAMANNA. Wait!

PARVIN. What?

THAMANNA. There's a fifth option.

RAJNA. Really?

PARVIN. What?

THAMANNA. Tell Salim the truth.

SABINA. What?

PARVIN. Why?

RAJNA. And?

THAMANNA. And see if he'll marry her anyway.

SABINA. What? And bring up another man's kid? Are you mad?

PARVIN. No chance.

SABINA. Uh-uh.

RAJNA. Forget it.

THAMANNA. Why not?

SABINA. Because – because everything!

THAMANNA. But I thought this was about being grown up! That is the grown-up thing to do. Be honest. Treat Salim with respect. Give him the choice at the very least. He's a good guy. I love him. He deserves that.

RAJNA. She's got a point.

PARVIN. He'd never agree to it.

RAJNA. You don't know that.

THAMANNA. There's a chance.

PARVIN. Really?

RAJNA. Oh my God.

THAMANNA. I don't know what you do to him, Parv, but he is *so* into you.

RAJNA. I can't believe we didn't see that before.

PARVIN. But that is – that is –

THAMANNA. Yeah. He'd be saving your life.

Small pause.

PARVIN. I don't know if I could do that to him.

RAJNA. It's better than lying.

PARVIN. But is it? Is it really?

RAJNA. Listen. I love you guys, and I love my family, and I love my community. I am proud of who I am and where I come from. So proud. But the secrets. My God, the secrets. Sometimes I think they're gonna drown us all. (*Quoting.*) 'Secrets are the stones that sink the boat. Take them out, look at them, throw them out, float.'[21]

PARVIN. Who said that?

RAJNA. Lemn Sissay. Legend.

THAMANNA. He came into our school!

RAJNA. Yeah. Yeah, he did. Sabina?

SABINA. What?

RAJNA. Gone quiet. What you thinking?

Pause.

SABINA. I'm thinking that life isn't like poetry, Rajna. I see it on my blog. Girls live their lives by song lyrics, then come crying to me.

RAJNA. I just think... out of everything, this is the most honourable thing to do.

SABINA. Yeah? And what if he says no? We're screwed. The secret's out, and then what?

RAJNA. We'd have done the right thing.

THAMANNA. Yeah.

SABINA. What – you really gonna change the whole community by coming clean about this one thing? You're a romantic, Rajna. You think you're a realist but you're not. None of you are. You're little girls, living life like a song.

RAJNA. That's not fair. We're being really strong here.

SABINA. Okay, so what about Tham's parents? Are they in on it too? Or is it just Salim, having his love exploited? Go Tigers! Kidding yourselves you're making a difference to anyone but yourselves.

RAJNA (*quietly*). It's one step at a time, Sabina.

Pause.

PARVIN. I know what this is about. It's cos you'd still be the secret auntie, isn't it?

SABINA. All I know is that it's funny how Thamanna suggested this, but she also stands to get the most out of it.

Pause.

THAMANNA. I am – *really* hurt that you would say that.

PARVIN. Guys, could I have a minute with Sabina? Just us.

RAJNA *and* THAMANNA *exchange glances then go*.

You're hurting. I can understand that.

SABINA. It's like… like you're making me choose. You over him. All of you – over him. My family. My blood.

PARVIN. Friends are the family you choose.

SABINA. That's a teenager talking. You know it ain't that simple.

PARVIN. Look, Sab, I'm not gonna try and persuade you one way or the other. All I'm gonna say is that you can't carry on being the person you are. None of us can. Whatever happens, this changes everything.

SABINA. Oh! I can make this go away. I can make *you* go away!

PARVIN. No, Sab, you can't. Because it's happening.

SABINA. Why did I have to write it like this?

PARVIN. Because it's the truth.

SABINA. When I was little, I used to love this story about the Underworld. About a girl descending to Hell to make sacrifices for the ones she loves. Now I realise the Underworld is where we all live, as adults. This dark world of fear and shame.

PARVIN. It's as dark as you make it, Sabina. Friendship, love – that's what lights it up.

SABINA *hugs* PARVIN.

SABINA. Oh, Parv. There's so much of me in you.

PARVIN. You always say that. What does it mean?

SABINA *puts her hand on* PARVIN*'s face*.

SABINA. One day, when you're older, you'll work it out.

Small pause.

PARVIN. What was the little girl about, Sabina?

SABINA. I don't know. She just appeared.

PARVIN. What does she mean?

SABINA *doesn't answer. She wipes away tears.*

I have to go now.

SABINA. Where?

PARVIN. Back home.

SABINA. Why?

PARVIN. To wait.

SABINA. Wait for what?

PARVIN. For you to write the ending.

PARVIN *pecks* SABINA *on the cheek.*

You'll be fine. We're so proud of you, you know. You carry us all.

PARVIN *goes.*

SABINA. And with that, we went to Salim, and we told him the truth.
It was hard
Two days of talking and tears.
But we told him everything
About camping
About the little girl
About what we'd been through – together.
We reached out
Held him close until the pain subsided;
We made him one of us.
Then, on the third day, he said yes.
He said: 'Yes.'
And in that moment, we saw something flicker;
His sacrifice stirred the fire in Parvin's heart.
We gathered round, and warmed our hands upon the future.

Time passes
Days, weeks, months slip by like landscapes on a train.
Rajna starts her MPhil and begins teaching.

RAJNA. In all religious societies, women and their sexual purity have been linked with the honour of men and families. This nexus transcends the terrain of any one religion...

SABINA. Thamanna's love interest gets an eighteen-month stretch –

THAMANNA. No way!

SABINA. But she soon forgets about him when she gets through the first round of *X Factor*.

THAMANNA *sings an opening line from a pop song*.[22]

Though she crashes out in round two.

THAMANNA. I don't believe it, Dermot!

SABINA. I get my own column: 'London Lives'
While Parvin and Salim's wedding goes without a hitch
The bond between them strengthened by a secret.

PARVIN *appears, heavily pregnant*.

Eight months later
We gather by her side as her waters break.

PARVIN. Oh God.

SABINA. And with them breaks a little piece of all our hearts.

The sound of an ambulance, and a flashing blue light.

RAJNA. Breathe in!

THAMANNA. Breathe out!

SABINA. The ambulance is on its way.

RAJNA. How far apart?

PARVIN. Oh God. Oh God.

RAJNA. Parvin, how far apart?

PARVIN. Five minutes, maybe less.

RAJNA. Call them back.

SABINA. They're round the corner.

PARVIN. Don't leave me!

RAJNA. We won't, sweetheart, I promise we won't.

They gather round PARVIN *in the ambulance.*

SABINA. In the ambulance
    Racing through East London
    Streets as smudged as our eyeliner
    I think I see something
    Pass something
    And my heart bolts out of my chest like a bird from a tree
    The girl!

RAJNA. What?

SABINA. The little girl!

THAMANNA. What girl?

SABINA (*to audience*). Standing at the entrance to the alley!
    Kinder Street, just off the main road!
    And waving!
    In that same flowery dress!
    Waving at us as we fly past!
    Stop!

RAJNA. What?

SABINA. Stop the ambulance!

PARVIN. I'm in labour!

SABINA. Oh yeah. Sorry.

    (*To audience.*) But as we screech into A and E
    And load Parvin onto a stretcher
    Something pulls me back
    Back to the alley
    I have to go
    Have to see.

THAMANNA. See what?

RAJNA. Where you going?

PARVIN. Don't leave me!

SABINA. I'll be back – I promise I'll be back.

THAMANNA. Sab, don't do this, don't freak out on us now!

SABINA. I'm not!

RAJNA. We've come this far!

SABINA. There's just something I have to do – please!

(*To audience*.) And I'm gone
Out the main gates
Screaming onto Whitechapel Road
Heart trying to outrun my legs
Hard left onto New Road
Nearly bouncing off car bonnets as I head south
Newark, Varden, Nelson
The street names like a sprint through history
Rocketing over Commercial Road
And splatting into the wall of Kinder Street like some dumb
cartoon
The girl!
The girl!
…Is nowhere to be seen.
She was here!
You were here!
Turning over bins
Checking over fences
In skips
Around corners
But nothing
Nothing
No one.

The faint sound of a little GIRL *laughing, echoey, distant,
bouncing off the walls of the alley.*

I head back to the main road
And stand
Eyes streaming
Lungs heaving
Coughing up dust like little pieces of the past
And it's then that I realise
I gotta make a choice.

Turn left – for home, my brother, and my mum.
Or turn right – for the hospital, the baby, and my best
friends.

And so I stand
Frozen
For what seems like for ever
Heart being savaged down the middle
Civilisations rise and fall around me
Not one of them as seething or as tangled or as deep
As what I'm feeling now.

She recites a prayer.

O Allah! I seek guidance by Your knowledge
I seek ability by Your power
I ask You of Your great bounty.
You have power, I have none.
You know, I know not.
You are the Knower of hidden things.[23]

I open my eyes
And though the sun is shining
I see four drops of rain
Falling
Falling
Like molten stars

*She puts out her right hand, palm upwards, as if catching
them.*

Four drops
And they land
One on each fingertip
Winking gently
Before running down each finger
Four tiny streams
Streaking my skin
And merging into one
In the valley of my right palm.

She closes her fingers around them.

And I know exactly which way to go.

The sound of a baby crying.

Someone hands SABINA *an open laptop.*

She takes it as if she has been typing this whole time.

I'm gonna put a full stop there
Because for now
It's over
Even though
It ain't never over.

But looking out my window
At the concrete world
It's just nice to know
That the forest is out there
It's always out there
If we ever need it again.

Rule Thirteen: Be brave enough to live creatively. It's the one true place where no one has ever been. You have to leave comfort behind, and head into the wilderness. But what you discover will be amazing. What you discover will be yourself.

She closes the laptop.

Fade to black.

The End.

1. In the 2010 production, the first line from Cheryl Cole's 'Parachute'

2. In the 2010 production, the first line from Christina Aguilera's 'Dreamy Eyes' (though any pop song lyric with the word 'eyes' in it would do)

3. 'God has willed it' – Arabic. Used to express appreciation, joy or praise of an aforementioned person or thing

4. Inner London pronunciation of 'settle'

5. 'In the name of God, the most Gracious, the most Merciful' – Arabic

6. A Muslim dua (prayer) traditionally said to ward off evil

7. 'Amen' – Arabic

8. 'Thank God!' – Arabic

9. 'God' – Arabic. Said in exclamation, like 'Oh God!' in English

10. Spirit being, a widespread belief among Muslims

11. 'Do you speak Bengali?' – Sylheti

12. 'What's your name?' – Sylheti

13. In the 2010 production, the first two verses of Beyoncé's 'If I Were a Boy', though any modern pop song with a lullaby quality would work

14. 'It's alright! You can come back now!' – Sylheti

15. 'Nothing' – Sylheti

16. 'Mum' – Sylheti

17. 'Dad' – Sylheti

18. 'Auntie' – Sylheti

19. 'Grandma' – Sylheti

20. 'God Willing' – Arabic

21. From *Something Dark* by Lemn Sissay, used with kind permission

22. In the 2010 production, JLS's 'One Shot'

23. Traditional Muslim dua said in times of difficulty